PREPARATION
FOR
DEATH

PREPARATION
FOR
DEATH

CONSIDERATIONS
ON THE ETERNAL MAXIMS

USEFUL FOR ALL AS MEDITATIONS, AND SERVICEABLE
TO PRIESTS FOR SERMONS

By

ST. ALPHONSUS MARIA DE LIGUORI

BISHOP OF ST. AGATHA, AND FOUNDER OF THE CONGREGATION OF THE
MOST HOLY REDEEMER

Newly Translated from the Italian
and edited by
ROBERT A. COFFIN, C.SS.R.
LATE BISHOP OF SOUTHWARK

TAN Books
Charlotte, North Carolina

Imprimatur: N. Card. Wiseman
               May 1, 1867

Originally published in 1857 by Burns, Oates and Washbourne, Ltd., London, England. Reprinted in 1972 by Marian Publications, South Bend, Indiana.

ISBN: 978-0-89555-174-0

Cover design by Milographics, milo.persic@gmail.com.

Cover photo: Mary wipes the tears from the face of Jesus. Photo © Sean Warren; iStockphoto.

Printed and bound in the United States of America.

TAN Books
Charlotte, North Carolina
1982

RESCRIPT OF HIS HOLINESS PIUS IX
(Translation)

"MOST HOLY FATHER,

"The Bishop of Southwark in England, in representing to your Holiness how the Redemptorist Fathers have had the consolation to see an immense good result from the condescension with which your Holiness was pleased to praise the *German* edition of the works of St. Alphonsus, humbly begs to be authorised to bless, in the name of your Holiness, the translation already commenced, and in part published, of the pious works of St. Alphonsus in *English.*"

"In an audience with his Holiness on the 13th of November 1853, our most holy Lord, by Divine Providence, Pope Pius IX, at the request of me, the undersigned Secretary of the Sacred Congregation for the Propagation of the Faith, was graciously pleased to grant the above petition; charging, however, the conscience of the petitioner with faithfulness in the translation.

"Given at Rome, from the Palace of the Sacred Congregation, on the day and in the year as above.

"Gratis, &c. &c.   —A. BARNABO, Secretary."

Contents

TO

MARY,

IMMACULATE AND EVER VIRGIN,

FULL OF GRACE, AND BLESSED ABOVE ALL THE CHILDREN OF ADAM,

THE DOVE, THE TURTLE-DOVE, THE BELOVED OF GOD

THE HONOR OF THE HUMAN RACE, THE DELIGHT OF

THE MOST HOLY TRINITY:

ABODE OF LOVE, MODEL OF HUMILITY,

MIRROR OF ALL VIRTUES:

MOTHER OF FAIR LOVE, MOTHER OF HOPE,

MOTHER OF MERCY:

ADVOCATE OF SINNERS, DEFENCE AGAINST THE DEVILS,

LIGHT OF THE BLIND, PHYSICIAN OF THE SICK:

ANCHOR OF CONFIDENCE, CITY OF REFUGE,

GATE OF PARADISE:

ARK OF LIFE, RAINBOW OF PEACE,

HAVEN OF SALVATION:

STAR OF THE SEA, AND SEA OF SWEETNESS

PEACEMAKER OF SINNERS, HOPE OF THE DESPAIRING,

HELP OF THE ABANDONED:

COMFORTER OF THE AFFLICTED, CONSOLATION OF THE DYING,

AND JOY OF THE WORLD,

HER AFFECTIONATE AND LOVING,
THOUGH VILE AND UNWORTHY SERVANT,
HUMBLY CONSECRATES THIS WORK

Preparatory Prayer

COME, Holy Ghost, fill the hearts of Thy faithful and kindle in them the fire of Thy love.

V. Send forth Thy Spirit, and they shall be created;

R. And Thou shalt renew the face of the earth.

Let us pray.

O God, who didst teach the hearts of Thy faithful people by sending them the light of Thy Holy Spirit, grant us by the same Spirit to have a right judgment in all things, and evermore to rejoice in His holy comfort. Through Christ our Lord. Amen

PREPARATION FOR DEATH

Object of the Work: Necessary to be Read

Some persons desired of me a book of considerations on the eternal truths for such souls as wish to establish themselves more firmly, and to advance in a spiritual life: others required of me a collection of subjects adapted for missions and spiritual exercises. That I might not multiply books, labor, and expense, I determined to write the present work according to the following method, that it may serve both purposes. To make it useful for meditation to those who live in the world, I have divided these considerations into three points. Each point will form a meditation; and after each point, therefore, I have added affections and prayers. I beg of the reader not to be weary, if in these prayers he always finds petitions for the grace of perseverance and the love of God, since these are the two graces most necessary for obtaining eternal salvation. "The grace of divine love is that grace," says St. Francis of Sales, "which contains in itself every grace, because the virtue of charity towards God brings with it all other virtues." "All good things came to me together with her." (*Wis.* 7:11). Whoever loves God is humble, chaste, obedient, mortified, and, in fine, possesses every virtue. St. Augustine says: "Love God, and do what thou wilt;" yes, because he who loves God will endeavor to avoid everything that is displeasing to Him, and will seek solely to please Him in all things.

1

The other grace, of perseverance, is that which enables us to obtain eternal life. St. Bernard says, "that Heaven is promised to those who commence a good life; but it is given only to those who persevere."[1] But this perseverance, according to the holy Fathers, is given only to those who ask for it. Hence St. Thomas asserts, "that in order to enter Heaven, it is necessary for a man after Baptism to pray continually."[2] And our Saviour had already said: "We ought always to pray, and not to faint." (*Luke* 18:1). Neglecting this, many miserable sinners, after receiving pardon, do not continue in the grace of God; they are forgiven, but because they omit to ask of God the grace of perseverance, especially in time of temptation, they fall again. On the other hand, although the grace of perseverance is entirely gratuitous, and cannot be merited by any good works of our own, F. Suarez nevertheless declares that it is infallibly obtained by prayer; St. Augustine having already said "that the gift of perseverance may be merited by supplication, that is, may be obtained by prayer."[3] We will prove at length this necessity of prayer in another little work, which is already in press, and will soon be published, entitled *On Prayer, as the great means, etc.* *—a work which, although short, and consequently not expensive, has nevertheless cost me much labor, and I consider it highly useful for every sort of person: I say moreover unhesitatingly, that among all spiritual treatises there is not, nor can be, one which is more useful or more necessary than this on prayer as the means for obtaining eternal salvation.

In order that the present Considerations may be useful also to such priests as have but few books, or who have no leisure for reading, I have added texts from Scripture and passages from the holy Fathers; short indeed, but strong—such as they ought to be for sermons. I must observe, that each Consideration, with the three points, forms a sermon. For this end I have

---

* In the vol. *Christian Virtues* of the present translation.—Editor

endeavored to collect from several authors such strik-
ing sentiments as appeared to me most calculated to
touch the heart; and I have inserted various such in
brief, that the reader may select those that please him,
and enlarge upon them afterwards at his pleasure.
May all redound to the glory of God! I entreat my read-
ers to recommend me to Jesus Christ, whether I be
dead or alive, when they shall read this book; and I
promise to do the same for all those who do me this
charity. Live Jesus our love, and Mary our hope.

CONSIDERATION I

Portrait of a Man Who has Recently Passed Into the Other World

"Dust thou art, and to dust thou shalt return."   Genesis 3:19

FIRST POINT

Consider that thou art dust, and to dust thou shalt
return. The day will come when thou shalt die, and
rot in a grave, where "worms shall be thy covering."
(*Isaias* 14:11). The same fate awaits all, high and low,
the prince and the peasant. As soon as the soul shall
have left the body, with the last gasp it will go into
eternity, and the body will return to dust. "Thou shalt
take away their breath, and they shall return to their
dust." (*Psalms* 103:29). Picture to yourself a person
who has recently expired. Behold that corpse lying on
the bed, the head fallen on the chest, the hair disordered and bathed in the sweat of death, the eyes sunken,
the cheeks hollow, the face of an ashy hue, the tongue
and the lips the colour of lead, the body cold and heavy.
The beholders grow pale and tremble. How many at
the sight of a deceased parent or friend have changed
their life and left the world! But still more horrible is

it when the body begins to decay. Twenty-four hours
have not elapsed since the death of that youth, and
an offensive odor is already perceptible. The windows
must be opened, and incense must be burnt, and haste
be made to transfer the body to the church and to bury
it, that the whole house may not be infected. "And if,"
says an author, "that body has belonged to one of the
great or the rich ones of the earth, it will only send
forth a more intolerable stench."

Behold to what that proud, that voluptuous man is
come! The favorite, the desired one of society, now become the horror and the abomination of all who behold
him. His relations hasten to remove him from the house,
and people are hired to bear him away, that, enclosed
in a coffin, they may cast him into a grave.

Formerly he was renowned for his talents, his ele-
gance, his graceful manners, and his wit; but no sooner
is he dead than he is forgotten. "Their memory hath
perished with a noise." (*Psalms* 9:7). On hearing the
news of his death, some say he was an honor to his
family; others, he has provided well for his family; others grieve because the departed had done them some
service; some rejoice because his death brings some
advantage to them. However, in a short time no one
will name him any more; and even from the very first
his dearest friends will not hear him mentioned, that
their grief may not be renewed. In the visits of con-
dolence other things are talked of; and if anyone should
chance to allude to the departed, the relations exclaim:
"For mercy sake, never name him to me."

Consider that, as you have done at the death of your
friends and relations, so others will do by you. The living appear upon the stage to occupy the wealth and
the places of the dead, and of the dead little or no
esteem or mention is any more made. At first the relations are afflicted for some days; but they quickly console themselves with that share of property which falls
to them, so that in a short time they will rejoice at
your death, and in that very room where you have

breathed forth your soul, and have been judged by Jesus Christ, they will dance, eat, play, and laugh, as before. And your soul, where will it then be?

AFFECTIONS AND PRAYERS

O Jesus, my Redeemer, I return Thee thanks for not having taken me out of this life whilst I was Thy enemy. How many years have passed since I deserved to be in Hell! Had I died on such a day, or on such a night, what would have become of me for all eternity? My God, I return Thee thanks. I accept of death as a satisfaction for my sins, and I accept of it in the manner in which it may please Thee to send it to me; but since Thou hast waited for me until now, oh, wait for me yet a little longer. "Suffer me, therefore, that I may lament my sorrow a little." (*Job* 10:20). Give me time to weep over my offenses against Thee, before Thou comest to judge me.

I will no longer resist Thy calls. Who knows but these words which I have just read are Thy last call to me? I acknowledge that I do not deserve mercy: Thou hast pardoned me so often, and I have again ungratefully offended Thee. "A contrite and humble heart, O God, thou wilt not despise." (*Psalms* 4:19). Ah, Lord, since Thou canst not despise a humble and penitent heart, behold the traitor who, humbled and repentant, has recourse to Thee. "Cast me not away from thy face." (*Psalms* 1:13). Thou hast said: "Him that cometh to me I will not cast out." (*John* 6:37). It is true that I have offended Thee more than others, because I have been favored more than others with light and grace; but the Blood Thou hast shed for me gives me courage, and proffers pardon to me if I repent. Yes, O my Sovereign Good, I do repent with my whole soul for having insulted Thee. Pardon me, and give me grace to love Thee for the future. I have long enough offended Thee. As for the remainder of my life, no, my Jesus, I will not spend it in offending Thee; I

will spend it wholly in weeping over the displeasure
I have given Thee, and in loving Thee with all my
heart, O God, worthy of infinite love. O Mary, my hope,
pray to Jesus for me.

SECOND POINT

But, that thou mayest more clearly see what thou
art, O Christian soul, says St. John Chrysostom, "go
to a sepulchre; contemplate dust, ashes, worms—and
sigh!" Behold how that corpse first becomes yellow,
and then black. Afterwards the whole body is covered
with a white and disgusting mold. Then there issues
forth a clammy, fetid slime, which flows to the earth.
In that corruption a multitude of worms are gener-
ated, which feed on the flesh. The rats feast on the
body; some on the outside, others enter into the mouth
and bowels. The cheeks, the lips, and the hair, fall to
pieces; the ribs are first laid bare, then the arms and
the legs. The worms, after having consumed all the
flesh, devour each other; and at last nothing remains
of that body but a fetid skeleton, which in time crum-
bles in pieces; the bones separate, and the head falls
from the trunk. "They became like the chaff of a summer's threshing-floor, and they were carried away by
the wind." (*Dan.* 2:35). See, then, what man is—a little dust on the barn floor, which is carried away by
the wind.

Behold that nobleman, who was called the life and
the soul of society—where is he? Enter into his room;
he is not there. If you look for his bed, it belongs to
others; if for his clothes, or his arms, others have already
taken and divided them amongst themselves. If you
would see him, go to that grave, where he is changed
into corruption and fleshless bones. O God, that body,
nursed with so many delicacies, clothed with such pomp,
waited upon by so many attendants—to what is it now
reduced! O ye Saints, you knew how to mortify your
bodies for the love of that God whom alone you loved

on this earth; and now your bones are preserved and prized as sacred relics in golden shrines, and your beauteous souls are in the enjoyment of God, in expectation of the last day, on which your bodies also shall be made their companions in glory as they have been partakers of the Cross in this life. This is true love of the body, to load it with mortifications here, that it may be happy in eternity; and to deny it those pleasures which will render it unhappy in eternity.

AFFECTIONS AND PRAYERS

Behold, then, O my God, to what my body will be reduced—that body which has so much offended Thee!—to worms and rottenness. But this does not afflict me, O my Lord; on the contrary, I rejoice that this my flesh, which caused me to lose Thee, my Sovereign Good, will rot and be destroyed; that which afflicts me is, that for the sake of wretched pleasures I have so much displeased Thee. But I will not distrust in Thy mercy. Thou hast waited for me, that Thou mightest pardon me. "Therefore the Lord waiteth, that he may have mercy on you." (*Isaias* 30:18). And Thou wilt pardon me if I repent. Yes, I repent with all my heart, O Infinite Goodness, of having despised Thee. I will say to Thee, with St. Catherine of Genoa, "My Jesus, no more sins, no more sins." No, I will no longer abuse Thy patience. Neither, O my crucified Love, will I wait to embrace Thee till Thou shalt be placed by my confessor in my hands at the hour of death: from this moment I embrace Thee, from this moment I recommend my soul to Thee. My soul has been so many years in the world without loving Thee; give me light and strength that I may love Thee during the remainder of my life. I will not wait till the hour of death to love Thee; from this moment I love Thee, I embrace Thee, I unite myself to Thee, and I promise never more to leave Thee. O most holy Virgin, bind me to Jesus Christ; and obtain for me that I may never lose Him more!

THIRD POINT

My brother, in this picture of death behold yourself, and what you will one day become: "Remember thou art dust, and to dust thou shalt return." Consider that in a few years, perhaps months or days, thou wilt become rottenness and worms. This thought made Job a saint: "I have said to rottenness, thou art my father; to worms, my mother and my sister." (*Job* 17:14).

All must come to an end; and if when you die your soul is lost, all is lost for you. "Consider thyself as already dead," says St. Lawrence Justinian, "knowing that thou must necessarily die."[4] If you were already dead, what would you not desire to have done? Now that you are alive, reflect that one day you, must die. St. Bonaventure says, "that to guide the vessel well, the pilot must place himself at the helm; thus, to lead a good life, a man must always imagine himself in death." Hence St Bernard says: "Look on the sins of youth, and blush; look on the sins of manhood, and weep; look on the present disorders of thy life, and tremble and amend." When St. Camillus de Lellis beheld the graves of the dead, he said to himself, "If these could live again, what would they not do for eternal life? And I who have time, what do I for my soul?" However, the Saint said this through humility. But as for you, my brother, perhaps you have reason to fear you are that barren fig tree of which our Lord said, "Behold, for these three years I come seeking fruit on this fig-tree, and I find none." (*Luke* 13:7). You, who for more than three years have been in the world, what fruit have you yielded? "Reflect," says St. Bernard, "that the Lord does not only seek flowers, but also fruit; that is, not only good desires and good resolutions, but also good works." Learn, then, how to profit of this time which God in His mercy gives you; do not wait to desire time to do well when there will be no more time, and it shall be said to you, "Time shall be no more: depart." Make haste, it is now time to leave this world; make haste, what is done is done.

AFFECTIONS AND PRAYERS

Behold me, O my God; I am that tree which for so many years has deserved to hear those words: "Cut it down; why cumbereth it the ground?" (*Luke* 13:7). Yes, because during all the years that I have been in the world I have brought forth no other fruit than the briers and thorns of sin. But, O Lord, Thou wilt not have me despair. Thou hast said to all, that whoever seeks Thee finds Thee: "Seek, and ye shall find." I do seek Thee, O my God, and I desire Thy grace. I grieve with my whole heart for all the offenses I have committed against Thee, and I wish I could die of sorrow for them. Hitherto I have fled from Thee; but I value Thy friendship more than the possession of all the kingdoms of the earth. I will no longer resist Thy calls. Thou wouldst have me all Thine; I give myself wholly to Thee, without any reserve. Thou hast given Thyself entirely to me on the Cross; I give myself entirely to Thee.

Thou hast said: "If you shall ask me anything in my name, that I will do." (*John* 14:14). My Jesus, trusting in this great promise, in Thy Name, and by Thy merits, I ask Thy grace and Thy love. Let Thy grace and Thy holy love abound in my soul, where sin has abounded I return Thee thanks for having given me grace to make this petition; since it is inspired by Thee, it is a sign that Thou wilt hear me. Favorably hear me, my Jesus; give me a great love for Thee, give me a great desire to please Thee, and the grace to accomplish this desire. O my powerful advocate Mary, do thou also hear me; pray to Jesus for me.

CONSIDERATION II

With Death All Ends

"The end is come—the end is come."
Ezechiel 7:2

FIRST POINT

Amongst worldlings, those only are esteemed happy who enjoy the goods, the pleasures, the riches, and the pomps of this world; but death puts an end to all these joys of earth. "For what is your life? it is a vapour, which appeareth for a little while." (*James* 4:15). The vapors which are exhaled from the earth, when raised in the air and clothed with the light of the sun, make a fair appearance; but how long does this beauty last? A breath of wind disperses it. Behold that nobleman, courted today, feared, and almost worshiped; tomorrow, when he is dead, he will be despised, reviled, and trampled upon. When death comes, we must leave all. The brother of that great servant of God, Thomas à Kempis, prided himself on having built a beautiful house; but he was told by a friend that it had one great defect. He inquired what that was. "The defect," replied the other, "is, that you have made a door in it." "What!" exclaimed he; "is a door a defect?" "Yes," said his friend; "for out of that door you will one day have to be borne forth dead, and thus leave house and all."

Death, in fine, deprives man of all the goods of this world. Ah, what a spectacle is it to behold a prince expelled from his palace, never more to enter it, and others take possession of his furniture, his money, and all his other goods! The servants leave him in his grave with hardly a garment to cover his body; there is no longer anyone to esteem or flatter him; neither are his last commands heeded. Saladin, who had acquired many kingdoms in Asia, gave orders, as he expired, that when his body was carried to the grave, a man should precede it with his shirt suspended to a pole, crying: "This is all that Saladin carries to the grave."

When the body of that prince is laid in the grave, the flesh falls off, and, behold, his skeleton can no longer be distinguished from other skeletons. "Go to the grave," says Basil, "and see if thou canst there discover who has been servant and who master." Diogenes was one day seen by Alexander the Great anxiously searching for something amongst the skulls of the dead. "What seekest thou?" inquired Alexander, with curiosity. "I seek," he replied, "the skull of King Philip thy father, and I cannot distinguish it from the rest; if thou canst find it, show it to me." "On this earth," observed Seneca, "men are born unequal; but after death all become equal." And Horace said: "Death levels the sceptre with the spade." In fine, when death comes, "the end comes"—all ends, and we have to leave all; of all the things of this world we carry nothing to the grave.

AFFECTIONS AND PRAYERS

My Lord, since Thou hast given me light to know that what the world esteems is all mere vapour and folly, give me strength to detach myself from it before death detaches me. Unhappy that I have been, how often have I offended Thee and lost Thee, the Infinite Good, for the miserable pleasures and possessions of this earth! O my Jesus, O my Heavenly Physician, cast Thine eyes upon my poor soul, look upon the many wounds I have inflicted upon myself by my sins, and have pity on me. I know that Thou canst and wilt heal me; but to be healed Thou desirest that I repent of the injuries I have done Thee. Yes, I do repent of them with all my heart: heal me, then, now that Thou canst heal me. "Heal my soul, for I have sinned against thee." (*Psalms* 40:5). I have forgotten Thee, but Thou hast not forgotten me; and now Thou makest me feel that Thou wilt also forget my past offenses against Thee if

I detest them. "But if the wicked do penance, I will
not remember all his iniquities." (*Ezech.* 18:21). Behold,
I now detest and abhor them above every evil; forget,
then, O my Redeemer, all the grief I have caused Thee.
In future, I will lose all, even life itself, rather than
Thy grace. And of what use to me are all the goods of
this world without Thy grace?

Ah, assist me; for Thou knowest how weak I am!
Hell will not cease to tempt me; already it prepares
for me a thousand assaults, to make me once more its
slave. No, my Jesus, do not forsake me. From this day
henceforth I will be the slave of Thy love. Thou art my
only Lord, Thou hast created me, Thou hast redeemed
me, Thou hast loved me beyond all others; Thou alone
deservest to be loved, Thee only will I love.

SECOND POINT

Philip II, king of Spain, being near his end, sent
for his son; and throwing away the royal robe, showed
to him his breast gnawed by worms, and then said
to him: "Prince, behold how we die, and how all the
grandeurs of this world end!" It was well said by
Theodoret, that "death fears neither riches, nor guards,
nor the purple;" and that "rottenness and corruption
flow from the bodies of princes as well as of vassals."
So that everyone that dies, even though he be a prince,
carries nothing with him to the grave; all his glory
remains on the bed on which he expires: "For when
he shall die, he shall take nothing away, nor shall his
glory descend with him." (*Psalms* 48:18). St. Antoninus
relates, that when Alexander the Great was dead, a
certain philosopher exclaimed: "Behold, he who yesterday trampled on the earth is now covered by the
earth. Yesterday the whole world did not suffice for
him, and now seven spans thereof is sufficient. Yesterday he led his armies over the earth, and now he
is conveyed by a few porters under it." But rather let
us hear what God says: "Why is earth and ashes

proud?" (*Ecclus.* 10:9). Man, seest thou not that thou
art dust and ashes? Of what art thou proud? Where-
fore do you waste your thoughts and years in aggrandising yourself in this world? Death will come, and
then all your greatness and all your projects will end:
"In that day all their thoughts shall perish." (*Psalms*
145:4). Oh, how much more happy was the death of
St. Paul the Hermit, who lived sixty years shut up
in a cave, than that of Nero, who lived emperor of
Rome! How much more happy was the death of St.
Felix, a Capuchin lay brother, than that of Henry
VIII, who lived in regal splendor, but the enemy of
God! We must reflect, however, that to obtain such a
death the Saints have left all things—country, pleasures, the hopes which the world held out to them—
and embraced a poor and despised life. They buried
themselves alive on this earth, that they might not
when dead be buried in Hell. But how can worldlings,
living in sin, amidst earthly pleasures and dangerous
occasions—how can they hope for a happy death?
God forewarns sinners that in death they shall seek
Him, and shall not find Him: "You shall seek me, and
shall not find me." (*John* 7:34). He says that then
will be the time for vengeance, not for mercy: "I will
repay them in due time." (*Deut.* 32:15). Reason tells
us the same, since at the hour of death a man of the
world will find himself weak in mind, his heart
obscured and hardened by evil habits, temptations
will be stronger; and how will he be able to resist at
the hour of death, who during life was so often and
so easily conquered? It would require then a greater
measure of Divine grace to change his heart; but is
God obliged to give him this grace? Has the sinner
merited it by the disorderly life he has led? And yet
it is a question of eternal happiness or eternal misery. How is it possible that, reflecting on this, he who
believes in the truths of faith does not leave all to
give himself entirely to God, who will judge us according to our works?

AFFECTIONS AND PRAYERS

Ah, Lord, unhappy that I am, how many nights have I lain down to sleep in enmity with Thee! O God, in what a wretched state was then my soul! It was hated by Thee, and it chose Thy hatred. Already was it condemned to Hell; nothing was wanting but the execution of the sentence. But Thou, O my God, Thou hast never ceased to seek me, and to offer me Thy pardon. But who can assure me that Thou hast as yet pardoned me? Must I, my Jesus, live in this fear till Thou hast judged me? Ah, the grief which I feel for having offended Thee! The desire I have to love Thee, above all Thy Passion! O my most dear Redeemer, make me hope that I am in Thy grace! I am sorry for having offended Thee, O my Sovereign Good; and I love Thee above all things. I resolve to lose all rather than lose Thy grace and Thy love. Thou wishest the heart that seeks Thee to rejoice: "Let the heart of them rejoice that seek the Lord." (*1 Par.* 16:10). Lord, I detest all my offenses against Thee, give me courage and confidence; reproach me no more with my ingratitude, since I myself know and detest it. Thou hast said that "Thou wilt not the death of a sinner, but that he be converted and live." (*Ezech.* 33:11). Yes, my God, I leave all, and turn to Thee; I seek Thee, I desire Thee, and I love Thee above all things. Give me Thy love, and I ask for nothing more. O Mary, thou art my hope; obtain for me holy perseverance.

THIRD POINT

David calls the happiness of this present life a dream of one awakening: "As the dream of them that awake." (*Psalms* 72:20). A certain author remarks thus upon these words: "A dream, because when the senses are at rest things appear great; and they are not, and soon vanish away." The goods of this world appear great, but in fact are nothing; like sleep, they last but a lit-

tle while, and then all vanishes. This reflection, that
with death all ends, caused St. Francis Borgia to resolve
to give himself wholly to God. The Saint had to accompany the body of the Empress Isabella to Granada.
When the coffin was opened, everyone fled from the
horrible sight and odor; but St. Francis, touched by
Divine light, remained to contemplate in that corpse
the vanity of the world; and gazing on it, exclaimed:
"Art thou, then, my empress? Art thou she before whom
so many great ones bent their knees in reverence? O
my mistress Isabella, where is thy majesty, where thy
beauty? Thus then," he concluded within himself, "end
the grandeurs and the crowns of this world! I will
therefore, from this day henceforth, serve a Master
who can never die." From that hour he dedicated himself wholly to the love of Jesus crucified; and he then
made a vow to become a religious, should his wife die;
which vow he afterwards fulfilled by entering the Society of Jesus.

Truly, then, did one disabused of the world write
these words on a skull: *Cogitanti vilescunt omnia.* He
who thinks of death cannot love the world. And, oh,
why are there so many unhappy lovers of this world?
Because they do not think upon death: "O ye sons of
men, how long will you be dull of heart? Why do you
love vanity, and seek after lying?" (*Psalms* 4:3). Miserable children of Adam, says the Holy Ghost, why do
you not banish from your hearts those many earthly
affections which make you love vanity and lies? That
which has happened to your forefathers will happen
also to you; they have inhabited your palace, they have
slept in that very bed, but now they are no longer
there: the same will happen to you. Therefore, O my
brother, give yourself quickly to God, ere death comes:
"Whatsoever thy hand is able to do, do it earnestly."
(*Eccles.* 9:10). That which you can do today, wait not
for tomorrow to do; for today passes and returns no
more; and tomorrow death may come upon you, so that
you can no longer do anything. Detach yourself quickly

from all that keeps you or may keep you from God. Let us renounce without delay all affection for these earthly goods before death forcibly robs us of them: "Blessed are the dead who die in the Lord." (*Apoc.* 14:13). Blessed are they who in dying are already dead in affection to this world. They do not fear death; they desire it; they joyfully embrace it; since it then, instead of separating them from the objects of their love, unites them to the Sovereign Good, who is alone beloved by them, and who will render them eternally happy.

AFFECTIONS AND PRAYERS

My dear Redeemer, I thank Thee for having waited for me. What would have become of me if I had died when I was far from Thee? Blessed forever be Thy mercy and Thy patience unto me during so many years. I thank Thee for the light and the grace with which Thou dost now assist me. I loved Thee not then, neither did I care much to be loved by Thee. Now I love Thee with my whole heart, and my greatest grief is to have thus displeased so good a God. This grief torments me; but sweet is the torment, since this grief gives me confidence that Thou hast already pardoned me. My sweet Saviour, oh, that I had died a thousand times rather than have ever offended Thee! I tremble lest in future I should again offend Thee. Ah, rather let me die the most painful death than again lose Thy grace! I have been the slave of Hell; but now, now I am Thy servant, O God of my soul. Thou hast said that Thou lovest those who love Thee: I do love Thee; then I am Thine, and Thou art mine. I may lose Thee in future; but this grace I ask of Thee, may I rather die than lose Thee again. Thou hast bestowed on me unasked so many graces, that I cannot fear being refused the grace which I now ask of Thee. Do not permit me ever again to lose Thee; give me Thy love, and I desire nothing more. Mary, my hope, intercede for me.

CONSIDERATION III

The Shortness of Life

*"What is your life? It is a vapour, which
appeareth for a little while."*

James 4:15

FIRST POINT

What is your life? It is like a vapor, which is dispersed by a breath of wind, and is no more. All know that they must die; but many are deceived by picturing to themselves death at such a distance as if it could never come near them. Job, however, bids us remember that the life of man is short: "Man's life is short: he cometh forth as a flower, and is destroyed." (*Job* 14:1, 2). The Lord commanded Isaias to preach this very truth: "Cry," He said to him, "all flesh is grass . . . indeed the people is grass. The grass is withered, and the flower is fallen." (*Isaias* 40:6, 7). The life of man is like the life of a blade of grass. Death comes, the grass withers, and behold life ends, and the flower falls of all greatness and all worldly goods.

"My days have been swifter than a post." (*Job* 9:25). Death comes to meet us more swiftly than a post, and we advance every moment towards death. In every step, in every breath we draw, we approach nearer to death. Even whilst I write, says St. Jerome, I approach nearer to death: "What I write is so much taken from my life." "We all die; and like the waters that return no more, we fall down into the earth." (*2 Kings* 14:14). Behold how the stream flows to the sea, and the flowing waters will return no more; thus, my brother, do your days pass away, and you approach to death; pleasures pass, amusements pass, pomp, praises, acclamations pass; and what remains? "The grave alone remains for me." (*Job* 17:1). We shall be cast into a grave, and there we shall have to remain, deprived of everything. At the hour of death, the remembrance of all the pleasures we have enjoyed in this life, and of all the honors we have acquired, will serve but to increase our diffidence as to obtaining eternal salvation. Then will the poor worldling exclaim: "Alas! my house, my gardens, that elegant furniture, those pictures, those garments, will soon be no longer mine: the grave alone remaineth for me." Alas, the goods of this earth are then only viewed with pain by those who have loved them with attachment; and this pain will still more endanger their salvation, since we find by experience that persons attached to the world will allow nothing to be mentioned but their ailments, the physicians that may be called in, and the remedies that may relieve them; and when the state of their souls is alluded to, soon do they weary, and bid you let them rest—for their heads ache, and they cannot bear to hear talking, and if sometimes they reply, they become confused, and know not what to say. Often does the confessor grant absolution, not because he knows them to be disposed for it, but because there is no time for delay. Thus do these die who think little upon death.

AFFECTIONS AND PRAYERS

Ah, my God, and Lord of infinite majesty! I am ashamed to appear before Thee. How many times have I dishonored Thee, preferring to Thy grace a filthy pleasure, an effusion of anger, a caprice, a little earth, a vapor! I adore and embrace, O my Redeemer, those holy wounds which I myself have inflicted on Thee by my sins; but through these very same wounds I hope for pardon and salvation. Make me comprehend, O my Jesus, the great injury I have done Thee in leaving Thee, the Fountain of all good, to drink of putrid and poisonous waters. What do I now reap from all my many offenses against Thee but sorrows, remorse of conscience, and fruits for Hell? "Father, I am not worthy to be called Thy son." (*Luke* 15:21). My Father, do not drive me from Thee. I no longer, indeed, deserve Thy grace, that I may become Thy son; but Thou hast died that I might be pardoned. Thou hast said: "Turn ye to me, and I will turn to you." (*Zach.* 1:3). I leave every gratification, I renounce all the pleasures that the world can give me, and I turn to Thee. Oh, pardon me by that blood Thou hast shed for me, since I repent with my whole heart of all my offenses against Thee. I repent, and I love Thee above all things. I am not worthy to love Thee, but Thou art worthy of being loved; accept of me to love Thee; do not disdain the love of that heart which once despised Thee. Thou didst spare me when I was living in sin, in order that I might love Thee. Yes; I will love Thee during the remainder of my life, and I will love Thee alone. Assist me, give me holy perseverance and Thy holy love. Mary, my refuge, recommend me to Jesus Christ.

SECOND POINT

King Ezechias said, with tears, "My life is cut off as by a weaver; whilst I was yet beginning, he cut me off." (*Isaias* 38:12). Oh, how many, whilst they are busy weaving—that is, preparing and executing the worldly projects which they have devised with such care—are surprised by death, which cuts all short! By the light of that last candle* all the things of this world vanish; applause, amusements, pomps, and grandeurs. Great secret of death, which makes us see that which the lovers of this world do not see! The most enviable fortunes, the most exalted dignities, the proudest triumphs, lose all their splendor when they are viewed from the bed of death. The ideas of certain false happiness, which we have formed to ourselves, are then changed into indignation against our own madness. The dark and gloomy shades of death cover and obscure all, even royal, dignities.

---

* In Catholic countries a blessed wax-taper is usually lighted and placed in the hand or by the bed of the dying.—Editor.

At present our passions make the things of this earth appear different from what they really are; death tears away the veil, and shows them in their true light, to be nothing but smoke, dirt, vanity, and misery. O God, of what use are riches, possessions, or kingdoms, in death, when nothing is needed but a coffin, and a simple garment to cover the body? Of what use are honors, when nothing remains of them but a funeral procession, and pompous obsequies, which will not avail the soul if it be lost? Of what use is beauty, if nothing remains of it but worms, stench, and horror, even before death, and after it a little fetid dust?

"He hath made me as it were a by-word of the people, and an example before them." (*Job* 17:6). That rich man, that minister, that general dies, and he will then everywhere be spoken of: but if he has led a bad life, he will become a by-word of the people; and, as a warning to others, he will be held up as an instance of the vanity of the world, and also of Divine justice. In the grave his body will be mingled with the corpses of the poor: "The small and great are there." (*Job* 3:19). What has the beautiful conformation of his body availed him, since now it is but a heap of worms? What has the authority he possessed availed him, since now his body is thrown into a grave to rot, and his soul has been cast into Hell to burn? Oh, what a misfortune, to serve for others as a subject for these reflections, and not to have made them to his own profit! Let us, then, be persuaded that the proper time for repairing a disordered conscience is not the hour of death, but during life. Let us hasten to do now that which we cannot do then. All passes quickly and ends. "The time is short;" therefore let us so act, that everything may serve us towards attaining eternal life.

AFFECTIONS AND PRAYERS

O God of my soul, O Infinite Goodness, have pity on me, who have so greatly offended Thee. I already knew that in sinning I should lose Thy grace, and I chose to lose it. Oh, tell me what I must do to regain it. If Thou desirest that I repent of my sins, I do indeed repent with my whole heart, and I wish I could die of grief. If Thou wilt that I hope for pardon, behold, I hope for it through the merits of Thy blood. If Thou wilt that I love Thee above all things, I leave all, I renounce all the pleasures and riches that the world can give me, and love Thee above every other good, O my most amiable Saviour. If, in fine, Thou desirest that I demand graces of Thee, I ask for two: permit me not to offend Thee anymore, and grant that I may love Thee; and then do with me as Thou wilt. Mary, my hope, obtain for me these two graces; I hope for them through thee.

THIRD POINT

What madness, then, for the sake of the wretched and brief pleasures of this short life to incur the risk of an unhappy death, and with it to commence a miserable eternity! Oh, how important is that last moment, that last gasp, that final closing of the scene! An eternity of every joy, or of every torment, is at stake—a life forever happy, or forever unhappy. Let us consider that Jesus Christ suffered a most bitter and ignominious death to obtain for us a happy death; and that He sends us so many calls, bestows on us so many lights, and admonishes us by so many threats, that at length we may be induced to conclude that last moment in the grace of God.

Even a pagan (Antisthenes), when asked what was most to be desired in this world, replied, "A good death." And what shall a Christian say, who knows by faith that at the moment of his death eternity begins; so that in that moment he grasps one of the two wheels which draws with it either eternal happiness or eternal suffering? If there were two tickets in a lottery, on one of which was written Hell, and on the other Heaven,

what care would you not take to find out how to draw
that of Heaven! O God, how do those unhappy wretches
tremble who are condemned to throw the dice upon
which depends their life or their death! What will be
your tears when you find yourself approaching that
last moment, in which you will say, "Upon this instant,
which is at hand, my eternal life, or eternal death,
depends. Now will be decided whether I shall be forever happy, or forever in despair." St. Bernardine of
Sienna relates of a certain prince, that, dying in great
terror, he exclaimed, "Behold, I have many estates, and
many palaces I have in this world; but if I die this
night, I know not what lodging will be mine."

My brother, if you believe that you must die, and
that there is an eternity, and that you can only die
once, so that if you then make a mistake, that mistake is forever and irremediable, how is it that you do
not resolve to begin from this very moment, in which
you read these words, to do all that you can to secure
to yourself a happy death? A St. Andrew Avellino said,
in trembling, "Who knows what will become of me in
the next world? Whether I shall be saved or damned?"
A St. Louis Bertrand likewise trembled, so as to be
unable to sleep during the night, when this thought
suggested itself, "Who knows but thou wilt be lost?"
And you, who have committed so many sins, do you
not tremble? Make haste, and amend in time; resolve
to give yourself truly to God, and begin from this time
at least a life which may not be an affliction, but a
consolation to you at the hour of death. Give yourself
to prayer; frequent the Sacraments; quit dangerous
occasions, and, if necessary, leave even the world; secure
your eternal salvation; and be convinced that to secure
this no precaution can be too great.

AFFECTIONS AND PRAYERS

O my dear Saviour, how great are my obligations to
Thee! And how couldst Thou bestow so many graces

upon one so ungrateful, upon such a traitor as I have been to Thee! Thou hast created me, and in creating me Thou didst foresee all the offenses I should commit against Thee. Thou didst redeem me by dying for me; and even then didst Thou foresee the ingratitude I should show towards Thee. When placed in this world, I turned away from Thee; and thus was I dead, till by Thy grace life was restored to me. I was blind, and Thou hast enlightened me. I had lost Thee, and Thou hast enabled me to find Thee. I was Thy enemy, and Thou hast made me Thy friend. O God of mercy, grant me to know my obligations to Thee, and to weep over my offenses against Thee. Ah, revenge Thyself upon me by giving me a great sorrow for my sins; but do not punish me by depriving me of Thy grace and Thy love. O Eternal Father, I abhor and detest above every evil the injuries I have done Thee. Have pity on me, for the love of Jesus Christ. Look on Thy Son, who died upon the Cross. "His Blood be upon me." May that Divine Blood descend upon my soul to cleanse it. O King of my heart, "Thy kingdom come." I am resolved to banish every affection that is not for Thee. I love Thee above all things; come and reign alone in my soul; grant that I may love Thee, and that I may love nothing but Thee. I desire to please Thee in all that I can, and to give Thee entire satisfaction during the remainder of my life. Do Thou bless, O my Father, this my desire, and give me the grace to keep myself always united to Thee. I consecrate all my affections to Thee, and from this day henceforth I will belong only to Thee, my Treasure, my Peace, my Hope, my Love, my All; I hope for everything from Thee, through the merits of Thy Son. My Queen and my Mother Mary, aid me by thy intercession. Mother of God, pray for me.

CONSIDERATION IV

Certainty of Death

"It is appointed unto men once to die."
Hebrew 9:27

FIRST POINT

The sentence of death is written against all men:
Thou art man, and thou shalt die. "Death alone is certain," said St. Augustine; "all other goods or evils are uncertain." It is uncertain whether the newborn infant will be poor or rich; whether it will have good or bad health; whether it will die young or old—all is uncertain; but it is certain it shall die. Nobles, monarchs, all will be cut off by death; and when death comes, no power can resist it. "We can resist fire, water, the sword; we can resist the power of princes; death comes—who can resist it?"[5] Belluacensis relates, that a certain king of France, the end of his life being come, said, "Behold, with all my power, I cannot induce death to wait for me one single hour more." When the end of life comes, it cannot be delayed, not even for an instant: "Thou hast appointed his bounds, which cannot be passed." (*Job* 14:5).

If then, dear reader, you should live all the years you reckon upon, still a day must come, and of that day an hour, which will be the last for you: for me who now write, for you who read this little book, already is the day and the moment decreed, on which I shall no longer write, nor you read: "Who is the man that shall live, and not see death?" (*Psalms* 88:49). The sentence is passed. There has never yet been a man so mad as to flatter himself that he should never die. That which has happened to your ancestors will happen to you also. Of all those who, at the beginning of the last century, lived in your country, behold, not one is living. Even the princes and monarchs of the earth have changed their abode; nothing remains of them but a marble mausoleum, with a grand inscription, which now only serves to teach us that all that is left of the great ones of this world is a little dust enclosed in a tomb. St. Bernard asks: "Tell me, where are the lovers of this world?" and he replies, "Nothing remains of them but ashes and worms."

Therefore, since our souls are immortal, we must strive, not for a temporal, but for an eternal gain. What would it avail you to be happy here (were it possible for a soul to possess true happiness without God), if afterwards you were to be unhappy for all eternity? You have built that house to your entire satisfaction; but reflect that soon you must leave it to rot in a grave. You have obtained that dignity which places you above others; but death will come, which will reduce you to the level of the meanest peasant on the earth.

AFFECTIONS AND PRAYERS

Ah, wretched that I am, who for so many years have done nothing but offend Thee, O God of my soul? Behold, those years have already passed away; death is, perhaps, already near; and what do I find in me but troubles and remorse of conscience? Oh, that I had always served Thee, my Lord! Fool that I have been, I have already lived so many years on this earth, and, instead of acquiring merits for another world, I have laden myself with debts to the Divine Justice. My dear Redeemer, give me light and strength now to settle my accounts. Death is, perhaps, not far from me. I wish to prepare myself for that great moment which will decide my eternal happiness or my eternal misery. I thank Thee for having waited for me till now; and since Thou givest me time to repair what I have done amiss, look upon me, O my God, and tell me what I must do for Thee. Dost Thou desire I should weep over my offenses against Thee? I do weep and lament over them with my whole soul. Dost Thou desire that I should spend the years or days that remain of my life in loving Thee? I will do so. O God, I have often before made the same resolution; but my promises have been deceitful. No, my Jesus, I will no longer be ungrateful for the many graces Thou hast bestowed on me. If now, at least, I do not change my life, how can I in death hope for pardon and Heaven? Behold, I now firmly resolve to begin to serve Thee in earnest. But do Thou give me strength, and do not forsake me. Thou didst not abandon me when I offended Thee; therefore I confidently rely upon Thy aid now that I purpose to leave all to please Thee. Accept me, then, to love Thee, O God, worthy of infinite love. Accept the traitor who now repentant embraces Thy feet, and loves Thee, and implores for mercy. I love Thee, my Jesus, I love Thee with my whole heart, I love Thee more than myself. Behold me, I am Thine. Dispose of me, and of all that belongs to me, according to Thy pleasure; give me perseverance in obeying Thee, give me Thy love, and then do with me what Thou wilt. Mary, my Mother, my hope, my refuge, to thee I recommend myself; to thee I consign my soul. Pray to Jesus for me.

SECOND POINT

"It is appointed." It is, then, certain that we are all condemned to death. "We are all born with the halter round the neck," says St. Cyprian; "and every step we take brings us nearer to death." My brother, as your name has been one day registered in the book of Baptism, so will it one day be registered in the book of death. As you now speak of your forefathers—the blessed memory of my father, of my uncle, of my brother—so will your successors say also of you. As you have often heard the bell toll for others, so will others hear it toll for you.

What would you say if you beheld a man condemned to death going to the scaffold jesting, laughing, looking about him, and thinking of plays, festivities, and amusements? And are you not now on your way to death? And of what are you thinking? Behold those in that grave, those friends and relations, on whom judgment has been already executed. What terror does it strike into those who are condemned to behold their companions suspended on the gallows! Look, then, at those corpses, each of which says to you, "Yesterday for me, today for thee." (*Ecclus.* 38:23). The same is said to you by the portraits of your deceased relations, their memoranda-books, their houses, their beds, the clothes they have left behind them.

What greater folly, then, can there be, than to know that we must die, and that after death an eternity of joy or an eternity of pain awaits us—to think that upon that moment depends our everlasting happiness or our everlasting misery—and yet not to think about settling our accounts, and taking every measure to secure a happy death! We pity those who die suddenly, and are not prepared for death; and why, then, do we not endeavor to keep ourselves prepared, since the same may happen to us? But, sooner or later, with warning or without it, whether we think of it or not, we must die; and every hour, every moment, we approach nearer to our gallows—that is to say, to that last illness which will send us out of the world.

In every age, houses, streets, and cities, are filled with new people, and the former ones are carried out to be enclosed in the tomb. As for those, the days of their life are ended; so will the time come when neither I, nor you, nor anyone now living, will exist any longer on this earth: "Days shall be formed, and no one in them." (*Psalms* 138:16). We shall then all be in eternity, which will be for us either an eternal day of delights or an eternal night of torments. There is no middle way; it is certain and of faith, that one or the other lot will be ours.

AFFECTIONS AND PRAYERS

My beloved Redeemer, I should not have the courage to appear before Thee did I not behold Thee hanging on this Cross, wounded, derided, and dead for my sake. My ingratitude has been great; but Thy mercy is still greater. My hope is in Thy wounds, Thy blood, Thy death. I merited Hell from the moment when I committed my first sin; since then how often have I again offended Thee; and not only hast Thou preserved my life, but in Thy great mercy and tender love Thou hast offered me pardon and peace: how, then, can I fear being rejected by Thee, now that I love Thee, and desire nothing but Thy grace? Yes, I love Thee with my whole heart, O my dear Lord, and I desire nothing but to love Thee. I love Thee; and I repent of having despised Thee, not so much because of the Hell that I have merited, as because I have offended Thee, my God, who hast so loved me. Come, O my Jesus, show me the tenderness of Thy Heart, and add mercy to mercy. Grant that I may never again be ungrateful to Thee; and wholly change my heart. Grant that this heart, which once valued not Thy love, and exchanged it for the miserable pleasures of this earth, may now be all Thine, and unceasingly burn with the flames of Thy love. I hope to gain Heaven, that I may love Thee forever; I cannot, indeed, have a place there amongst the innocent, my place will be with the penitent; but amongst those I will love Thee more than the innocent. For the glory of Thy mercy let Heaven behold a sinner, who has so greatly offended Thee, burning with an immense love. I resolve from this day henceforth to be all Thine, and to think of nothing but of loving Thee. Assist me, then, with Thy light and Thy grace, which will give me strength to accomplish this desire, which Thou givest me Thyself in Thy goodness. O Mary, thou who art the Mother of perseverance, obtain for me to be faithful to this my promise.

THIRD POINT

Death is certain. But, O God, Christians already know this; they believe it, they see it; and how, then, do so many live as forgetful of death as if they were never to die? If, after this life, there were neither Hell nor Heaven, could they think less of it than they do now? And therefore do they lead such bad lives. My brother, if you wish to live well, endeavor to live during the remainder of your life in the presence of death. "O death, thy judgment is good." (*Ecclus.* 41:3). Oh, how truly does he judge of things, and how well does he regulate his actions, who judges and regulates them with death before his eyes! The remembrance of death makes us lose all affection for the things of this life. "Reflect on the end of life, and there will be nothing in this world to love,"[6] says St. Laurence Justinian. "All that is in the world is the concupiscence of the flesh, and the concupiscence of the eyes, and the pride of life." (*1 John* 2:16). All the goods of the world are comprised in the pleasures of sense, in riches, and honors; but he thoroughly despises all who reflects that shortly he will be nothing but ashes, and buried under the earth to be food for worms.

And, in truth, with death present to them, the Saints have despised all the pleasures of this world. St. Charles Borromeo kept always on his table a skull, that he might continually contemplate it. Cardinal Baronius had these words inscribed on his ring: "Remember that you die—*Memento mori*." The venerable Father Juvenal Ancina, Bishop of Saluzzo, had this motto written on a skull, "What thou art I was; what I am thou shalt be." Another saint, a hermit, being asked at the hour of death why he was so joyful, replied: "I have always kept death before my eyes; and therefore, now that it is come, I see in it nothing new."

What folly would it not be in a traveler, if, whilst traveling, he were to think of aggrandising himself in that country through which he passed, without caring as to being reduced afterwards to live miserably in that in which he has to pass all his life! And is he not mad who seeks to be happy in this world, where he has only to remain a few days, and runs the risk of being unhappy in the next, where he will have to live for all eternity? He who possesses borrowed goods does not place his affections on them, because he knows that they will soon have to be returned. All the goods of this world are but lent us; it is folly to place our affections on them, since we must so soon leave them. Death will deprive us of everything. All the gains and riches of this world terminate in a dying gasp, a funeral, and a descent into the grave. The house you have built must ere long be given up to others; the tomb will be the habitation of your body till the day of judgment, and from thence it will pass to Heaven or Hell, where the soul will have already preceded it.

Affections and Prayers

In death, then, all will end for me. I shall only find, O my God, that little which I have done for the love of Thee. And what do I wait for? Do I wait for death to come and find me miserable and defiled with sin, as I now am? Were I now to die, I should die most uneasy and most dissatisfied with my past life. No, my Jesus, I will not die thus dissatisfied. I thank Thee for having given me time to weep over my sins, and to love Thee. I will begin from this moment. I grieve for having offended Thee, above every evil, O my Sovereign Good, and I love Thee above all things, more than my life. I give myself wholly to Thee; my Jesus, from this hour I embrace Thee, I clasp Thee to my heart; and from this moment I consign my whole soul to Thee: "Into Thy hands I commend my spirit." I will not wait to give it Thee until its departure from this world shall be announced to it, with that *Proficiscere*—Depart, O soul. I will not wait till then to implore Thee to save me. "O Jesus, be a Jesus to me!" My Saviour, save me

now, by pardoning me and giving me the grace of Thy
holy love. Who knows but this consideration, which I
have this day read, may be the last call Thou wilt send
me, and the last mercy Thou wilt show me? Extend
Thy hand to me, O my Beloved, and deliver me from
the mire of my tepidity; give me fervor; grant that I
may obey Thee with great love in all that Thou demand-
est of me. Eternal Father, for the love of Jesus Christ,
give me holy perseverance and the grace to love Thee,
and to love Thee greatly during the remainder of my
life. O Mary, Mother of mercy, by the love thou bearest thy Jesus, obtain for me these two graces—perseverance and love.

CONSIDERATION V

Uncertainty of the Hour of Death

"Be you then also ready; for at what
hour you think not, the Son of Man will
come."   Luke 12:40

First Point

It is certain that we shall all die; but when is uncertain. "Nothing" (says the author who styled himself
Idiota) "is more certain than death; and nothing is
more uncertain than the hour of death." My brother,
already is the year, the month, the day, the hour, and
the moment fixed in which you and I are to leave this
world and to enter into eternity; but this time is
unknown to us. In order that we may be always prepared, Jesus Christ now tells us that death "will come
furtively, like a thief in the night." (*1 Thess.* 5:2). Now
He tells us to watch, because he will come to judge us
when we least expect him. (*Luke* 12:40). God, for our
good, conceals from us the hour of our death, said St.
Gregory, that we may be always prepared to die: "We

are uncertain of death, that we may be always found prepared for it." Since death, then, may at any time, or in any place, rob us of life, we must, says St. Bernard, if we wish to die well, and to save our souls, expect it at every time and in every place: "Death waits for thee everywhere; do thou everywhere wait for it."

Everyone knows that he must die; but the evil is, that many regard death as so distant, that they lose sight of it. Even the most decrepit old men, and the most sickly persons, flatter themselves that they may still have three or four years more to live. But I, on the other hand, say, how many have we known, even in our own days, who have died suddenly; some sitting, some walking, some asleep in their beds! It is certain that none of these thought to die so suddenly, or on that day on which they died. I say moreover, that of the many who this very year have passed into the next world, dying in their beds, not one had imagined that his days were to end this year. Few are the deaths which do not come unexpectedly.

Therefore, dear Christian, when the devil tempts you to sin, saying that tomorrow you will go to confession, reply to him: And how do I know that this may not be the last day of my life? Should that hour, that moment, in which I turned my back to God, be the last for me, so that for me no time remained for reparation, what would become of me in eternity? To how many poor sinners has it happened, that in the very moment when they were feeding upon some poisoned bait, they were surprised by death, and sent to Hell: "As fishes are taken with the hook, so men are taken in the evil time." (*Ecclus.* 9:12). The evil time is precisely that in which the sinner actually offends God. The devil says that this misfortune will not befall you, but you ought to say: And should it befall me, what will become of me for all eternity?

AFFECTIONS AND PRAYERS

O Lord, the place in which at this moment I ought to be is not where I now am, but in that Hell which my sins have so often merited. "Hell is my house." But St. Peter declares that "the Lord waiteth patiently for your sake, not willing that any should perish, but that all should return to penance." (*2 Peter* 3:9). Thou hast, then, had so much patience with me, and waited for me, because Thou didst not wish me to be lost, but that I should return and do penance. Yes, my God, I return to Thee; I cast myself at Thy feet, and I implore Thy mercy: "Have mercy upon me, O God, according to Thy great mercy." Lord, it requires a great and extraordinary mercy to pardon me, because I have offended Thee in the midst of light. Other sinners also have offended Thee; but they have not had the light Thou hast given to me. Nevertheless, Thou commandest me to repent of my sins, and to hope for pardon from Thee. Yes, my dear Redeemer, I repent with all my heart of having offended Thee; and I hope for pardon through the merits of Thy passion. Thou, my Jesus, being innocent, hast chosen to die as a criminal on a cross, and to shed all Thy blood to wash away my sins. "O blood of the Innocent, wash away the sins of the penitent!" O eternal Father, pardon me for the love of Jesus Christ; hear His prayers, now that He intercedes for me, and makes Himself my advocate! But it is not enough for me to be pardoned, O God, worthy of infinite love; I desire also to love Thee. I love Thee, O Sovereign Good; and from this day henceforth I offer Thee my body, my soul, my will, my liberty. From this day I will avoid not only grievous, but even slight offenses against Thee. I will fly all dangerous occasions. "Lead us not into temptation." Deliver me, for the love of Jesus Christ, from those occasions in which I might offend Thee. "But deliver us from evil." Deliver me from sin; and then chastise me as Thou wilt. I accept of all the infirmities, pains, and losses which it may please Thee to

send me; it is enough for me not to lose Thy grace and
Thy love. Thou promisest to grant whatsoever is asked
of Thee. "Ask, and you shall receive." I ask of Thee
these two graces—holy perseverance, and the grace to
love Thee. O Mary, Mother of mercy, pray for me; in
thee do I put my trust.

SECOND POINT

The Lord desires not that we should be lost, and
therefore He ceases not to exhort us to change our life
by the threat of punishment. "Unless you be converted,
he will brandish his sword." (*Psalms* 7:13). Behold, He
says in another place, how many, because they would
not give up sin, have been surprised by death when
they least expected it, and were living in peace, secure
of many years to come: "For when they shall say, peace
and security, then shall sudden destruction come upon
them." (*1 Thess.* 5:3). In another place He says: "Unless
you shall do penance, you shall all likewise perish."
(*Luke* 13:3). Why so many warnings of punishment ere
He allows it to fall upon us? Why, but because He desires
our amendment, and thus that we should avoid an
unhappy death. Whoever says, Beware! does not wish
to kill thee, says St. Augustine: "He does not desire to
strike thee, who cries out to thee, take care."
We must, then, prepare our accounts before the day
of reckoning arrives. Dear Christian, if you were to die
this day before night, and the affair of your eternal life
were to be decided, what say you? Would you find your
accounts prepared? Or, rather, how much would you
pay to obtain from God another year, a month, or at
least another day? And why, now that God gives you
this time, do you not settle your conscience? Is it that
this day cannot be the last for you? "Delay not to be
converted to the Lord, and defer it not from day to day;
for his wrath shall come on a sudden, and in the time
of vengeance he will destroy thee." (*Ecclus.* 5:9). In order
to be saved, my brother, sin must be left. "If, then, you

must leave it at some time, why not leave it now?" says St. Augustine. Do you perchance wait the arrival of death; but for the obstinate death is not the time of pardon, but of vengeance: "In the time of vengeance He will destroy thee."

If anyone owes you a large sum, you quickly take care to provide yourself with a written security, saying, Who knows what may happen? And why, then, do you not take the same precaution for your soul, which is of much more consequence than that sum? Why not say the same, Who knows what may happen? If you lose that sum, you do not lose all; and even if in losing it you lost all your patrimony, still would the hope of regaining it remain; but if in death you lose your soul, then truly you will have lost all, and there will be for you no hope any more of recovering it. You are so careful in keeping accounts of your possessions, lest they should be lost if a sudden death were to befall you; and if perchance this sudden death were to happen to you, and you are in enmity with God, what would become of your soul for all eternity?

AFFECTIONS AND PRAYERS

Ah, my Redeemer, Thou hast shed all Thy Blood, Thou hast given Thy Life to save my soul; and I have so often lost it, hoping in Thy mercy: and thus I have often made use of Thy goodness, for what? To offend Thee more. I deserved to be struck dead for this, and to be cast into Hell. In fine, I have engaged in a contest with Thee: Thou in showing me mercy, I in offending Thee; Thou in coming after me, I in flying from Thee; Thou in giving me time to repair the ill done, I in making use of it to add injury to injury. O Lord, make me comprehend the great wrong I have done Thee, and the obligation that I am now under to love Thee. Ah, my Jesus, how could I be so dear to Thee, as that Thou shouldst so eagerly seek me, when I drove Thee away from me? How couldst Thou bestow so many

graces upon one who has so often displeased Thee? I
see by all this how desirous Thou art that I should
not be lost. I repent with all my heart of having offended
Thee, O Infinite Goodness. Ah, receive this ungrateful
sheep of Thy flock, returning penitent to Thy feet;
receive it and bind it on Thy shoulders, that it may
never more fly from Thee. No, I will not again abandon Thee; I will love Thee; I will be all Thine; and,
provided that I be Thine, I am content to endure every
pain. And what greater pain can befall me than to live
without Thy grace, separated from Thee who art my
God, who hast created me, and hast died for me? Ah,
accursed sins, what have you done? You have caused
me to offend my Saviour, who has so greatly loved me.
Ah, my Jesus, as Thou hast died for me, so ought I to
die for Thee; Thou hast died for love; I ought to die of
sorrow for having displeased Thee. I accept of death
in the way and at the time it pleaseth Thee; but hitherto I have not loved Thee, or loved Thee too little: I
will not die thus. Oh, grant me a little more time, in
order that I may love Thee before I die; change, therefore, my heart; wound it, inflame it with Thy holy love:
grant this through that charitable love which caused
Thee to die for me. I love Thee with my whole soul.
My soul is enamored of Thee. Do not permit that it
lose Thee any more. Give me holy perseverance; give
me Thy love. Most holy Mary, my refuge and my Mother,
oh, be my advocate.

Third Point

"Be ye ready." The Lord does not say, that we must
prepare ourselves when death arrives, but that death
must find us prepared. When death comes, it will be
almost impossible to settle a troubled conscience in
that tempest and confusion. Thus reason tells us.
Thus does God threaten, saying, that He will not
then come to pardon, but to avenge the contempt
shown of His graces: "Revenge is mine, I will repay

saith the Lord." (*Rom.* 12:19). "A just punishment," says St. Augustine, "will this be to him who, being able was not willing to save himself, that when he is willing he will not be able."⁷ But some will say: Who knows? It is possible I may then be converted and saved. But would you throw yourself into a well, saying: Who knows? It may be that throwing myself into it I may live, and not be killed. O God, how is this? How does sin darken the mind, which it deprives even of reason! When the body is concerned, men speak like sages; when the soul is concerned, like madmen.

My brother, who knows but this point which you read may be the last warning God sends you? Let us quickly prepare for death, that it may not overtake us suddenly. St. Augustine says, that the Lord hides from us the last day of our life, that we may every day be prepared to die: "The last day is hidden, that we may watch every day."⁸ St. Paul declares, that we must not only work out our salvation with fear, but with trembling: "Work out your salvation with fear and trembling." (*Phil.* 2:12). St. Antoninus relates, that a certain king of Sicily, in order to make one of his subjects understand with what fear he occupied the throne, caused him to sit at table with a sword suspended over his head by a slender thread, so that this man being thus situated could hardly taste any food. We are all in similar peril, since every moment the sword of death may fall upon us, and on it our eternal salvation depends.

Eternity is at stake. "If the tree fall to the south or to the north, in which place soever it shall fall, there shall it be." (*Ecclus.* 11:3). If when death comes we are found in the grace of God, oh, what joy for the soul to be able then to say: I have secured all, never again can I lose my God, I shall be forever happy! But should the soul be caught by death in sin, with what despair will she exclaim: Thus I have erred; and my error can never be repaired during all eternity! This fear caused the venerable Father Avila, the apostle of Spain, to

say, when death was announced to him: "Oh, had I but
a little more time to prepare myself to die!" This fear
made the Abbot Agatho say, although he died after so
many years of penance: "What will become of me? Who
knows the judgments of God?" St. Arsenius also trembled at the hour of death, and when asked by his disciples why he was in such fear, he replied, "My children,
this fear is not new to me; I have had it during my
whole life." More than all did holy Job tremble, saying, "What shall I do when God shall rise to judge?
And when he shall examine, what shall I answer him?"
(*Job* 31:14).

AFFECTIONS AND PRAYERS

Ah, my God, who has ever loved me more than Thou,
and whom have I ever despised and insulted more? O
Blood, O Wounds of my Jesus! You are my hope. Eternal Father, do not regard my sins; look upon the Wounds
of Jesus Christ; look upon Thy beloved Son, dying of
grief for me, and beseeching Thee to pardon me. I repent,
O my Creator, of having offended Thee; it grieves me
beyond any other evil. Thou hast created me that I
might love Thee, and I have lived as if Thou hadst created me to offend Thee. For the love of Jesus Christ,
pardon me, and give me grace to love Thee. Formerly I
resisted Thy will; now I will no longer resist it, I will
do all that Thou commandest. Thou commandest me to
detest the offenses I have committed against Thee;
behold, I detest them with all my heart. Thou commandest me to resolve never more to offend Thee; behold,
I resolve to lose my life a thousand times rather than
Thy grace. Thou commandest me to love Thee with all
my heart; yes, with all my heart I love Thee, and only
Thee will I love: from this day henceforth Thou shalt
be my only beloved, my only love. I ask of Thee, and I
hope from Thee, the gift of perseverance. For the love
of Jesus Christ, grant that I may be faithful to Thee,
and that, with St. Bonaventure, I may always say to

Thee, "My beloved is one; one only is my love." No, I am resolved that life shall no longer be spent in displeasing Thee; I desire to employ it only in weeping over the displeasure I have given Thee, and in loving Thee. Mary, my Mother, thou prayest for all those who recommend themselves to thee: pray to Jesus also for me.

CONSIDERATION VI

Death of the Sinner

"When distress cometh upon them, they will seek for peace, and there shall be none. Trouble shall come upon trouble."
Ezechiel 7:25, 26

FIRST POINT

At present sinners banish the remembrance and thought of death, and thus seek for peace (although they never find it) by leading a life of sin; but when they shall be in the agonies of death, about to enter into eternity, "when distress cometh upon them, they will seek for peace, and there will be none," then can they no longer fly from their evil conscience; they will seek peace, but what peace can be found by a soul laden with sins, which sting it like so many vipers? What peace, when he reflects that in a few moments he must appear before Jesus Christ his Judge, whose law and friendship he has hitherto despised? "Trouble shall come upon trouble." The announcement of death just received by him, the thought of bidding farewell to all the things of this world, the remorse of his conscience for the time lost, the time that is wanting, the rigor of Divine justice, the miserable eternity that awaits sinners; all these things will raise a terrible storm, which will confuse his mind, increase his apprehensions; and thus confounded and fearful, the dying man will pass into the other world.

Abraham, with great merit, hoped in God against all human hope, believing in the Divine promise: "against hope he believed in hope." (*Rom.* 4:18). But sinners, with great demerit, and falsely, to their own ruin, hope not only against hope, but also against faith, whilst they despise even the threats of God against the obstinate. They fear a bad death, but they fear not to lead an evil life. Yet, who assures them that they shall not die suddenly, by lightning, apoplexy or the bursting of a blood vessel? And even should they have time in dying to be converted, who assures them that they will be truly converted? St. Augustine had to combat for twelve years to overcome his bad habits; is it probable, then, that a dying man, who has always had a conscience stained with sin, will be truly converted in the midst of pains, distraction of mind, and in all the confusion of death? I say *truly,* because it is not enough to say and to promise, but we must say and promise from the heart. O God, with what terror will the miserable sufferer whose conscience has been neglected be seized and confounded, when he finds himself overwhelmed with sins, and fears of judgment, Hell, and eternity! Into what confusion will he be thrown by these thoughts, when he finds his head weak, his mind obscured and assailed by the pains of approaching death! He will confess, promise, weep; he will seek mercy from God, but without knowing what he does. And in this storm of agitation, remorse, grief, and terror, he will pass to the next world: "The people shall be troubled, and they shall pass." (*Job* 34:20). It is well said by a certain author, that the prayers, tears, and promises of the dying sinner are like the tears and promises of a man attacked by his enemy, who holds a dagger to his throat to rob him of his life. Unhappy he who lies down on his bed under the displeasure of God, and from thence passes into eternity.

AFFECTIONS AND PRAYERS

O Wounds of Jesus, you are my hope! I should despair of pardon for my sins, and of my eternal salvation, did I not look upon you, the fountains of mercy and grace, through which a God has shed all His Blood to wash my soul from the many sins I have committed. I adore you, then, O holy Wounds, and I trust in you. I detest a thousand times, and curse those unworthy pleasures by which I have displeased my Redeemer, and have miserably lost His friendship. Looking, then, upon you, I raise my hopes, and turn my affections towards you, my dear Jesus. Thou deservest that all men should love Thee and love Thee with all their heart; but I have so much offended Thee, and despised Thy love; and Thou notwithstanding hast borne with me so long, and with so much mercy invited me to pardon. Ah, my Saviour, do not permit that I should any more offend Thee, and lose my soul. O God, what torment should I endure in Hell at the sight of Thy Blood, and of the many mercies Thou hast shown me! I love Thee, and I will always love Thee. Give me holy perseverance. Detach my heart from all love that is not for Thee, and establish in me a true desire and resolution from this day henceforth to love only Thee, my Sovereign Good.

O Mary, my Mother, draw me to God, and make me wholly His ere I die.

SECOND POINT

Not one, but many, will be the torments of the dying sinner. On the one hand he will be tormented by devils. At the hour of death those horrible enemies exert all their strength to cause the loss of that soul which is about to quit this life; they know that but little time remains for them to win it, and that if they lose it then, they will have lost it forever: "The devil is come down unto you, having great wrath, knowing that he hath but a short time." (*Apoc.* 12:12). And not one, but innumerable, will be the devils who surround the dying man, to tempt him, and to bring him to perdition: "Their houses shall be filled with serpents." (*Isaias* 13:21). One will say to him, "Fear not, thou wilt recover." Another will say, "How is this? For so many years thou hast been deaf to the voice of God, and now dost thou expect Him to show thee mercy?" Another, "How canst thou now repair the injuries done, the reputations thou hast ruined?" Another, "Dost thou not perceive that all thy confessions have been null, without true sorrow, without purpose of amendment? How canst thou now repair them?"

On the other hand the dying man will behold himself surrounded by his sins: "Evils shall catch the unjust man unto destruction." (*Psalms* 139:12). "These sins," says St. Bernard, "like watchful guards, shall hold him in their grasp, and say to him: We are thy work, we will not leave thee; we will accompany thee into the next life, and we will present ourselves with thee to the Eternal Judge." The dying man will then wish to deliver himself from such enemies; but for this he must detest them. He must be converted with his whole heart to God; whereas his mind is darkened, and his heart hardened: "A hard heart shall fare evil at the last; and he that loveth danger shall perish in it." (*Ecclus.* 3:27). St. Bernard says, that the heart which has been obstinate in sin during life will use its utmost endeavors to escape damnation, but will not succeed, and overwhelmed by its own malice will end life in the same state. Having till then loved sin, the sinner has also loved the danger of being damned; justly therefore will the Lord permit him to perish in that danger in which he chose to live up to the time of his death. St. Augustine says, that he who is abandoned by sin, before he himself abandons it, will hardly detest it at the hour of death as he ought, because what he does then will be done through necessity: "He who is left by sin before he himself leaves it, does not condemn it of his own free will, but as it were by necessity."

Unhappy, then, the hardened sinner who resists the calls of God. Instead of yielding, and being softened by the voice of God, he ungratefully becomes more obdurate, as the anvil is hardened by the strokes of the hammer: "His heart shall be as hard as a stone, and as firm as a smith's anvil." (*Job* 41:15). His punishment will be to find himself the same in death, although on the point of passing into eternity: "A hard heart shall fare evil at the last." "Sinners," says the Lord, "have turned away from me for the love of creatures:" "they have turned their back to me, and not their face; and in the time of their affliction, they will say: Arise, and deliver us. Where are the gods whom thou hast made thee? Let them arise and deliver thee." (*Jer.* 2:27, 28). The unhappy wretches will have recourse to God in death, and God will say to them, "Now do you come to Me? Call upon creatures to help you, since they have been your gods." Thus will the Lord say, because they will have recourse to Him, but without a sincere intention of being converted. St. Jerome declares that he holds for certain, and has learnt from experience, that he will never make a good end who has led a bad life to the very last: "This I hold, this I have learned by much experience, that his will be an evil end who has always led an evil life."[9]

AFFECTION AND PRAYERS

My dear Saviour, help me, do not abandon me; I see my soul all covered with the wounds of sin, my passions do violence to me, bad habits overwhelm me; I cast myself at Thy feet, have pity on me, and deliver me from so many evils: "In Thee, O Lord, have I hoped: let me not be confounded forever." Do not permit that a soul trusting in Thee should be lost. I repent of having offended Thee, O Infinite Goodness; I have done evil, and confess it; cost what it may, I wish to amend;

but unless Thou assist me with Thy grace, I am lost.
Receive, O my Jesus, this rebel, who has so grievously
offended Thee. Remember that I have cost Thee Thy
blood and Thy life. Through the merits, then, of Thy
passion and death, receive me into Thy arms, and give
me holy perseverance. I was already lost; Thou hast
called me: behold, I will no longer resist; I consecrate
myself to Thee; bind me to Thy love, and do not permit me any more to lose myself, by losing again Thy
grace. My Jesus, do not permit it, Mary, my Queen, do
not permit it; rather obtain death for me, and a thousand deaths, than that I should again lose the grace
of thy Son.

THIRD POINT

Wonderful to say, God does nothing but threaten sinners with an unhappy death: "Then they shall call
upon me, and I will not hear." (*Prov.* 1:28). "Will God
hear his cry when distress shall come upon him?" (*Job*
27:9). "I also will laugh in your destruction, and will
mock." (*Prov.* 1:26). God laughs when He will not show
mercy.[10] "Revenge is mine, and I will repay them in
due time, that their foot may slide." (*Deut.* 32:35). In
so many other places He threatens the same; and yet
sinners live on in peace, as secure as if God had certainly promised them pardon and paradise. It is true,
that in whatever hour the sinner is converted, God has
promised to pardon him; but He has not said that in
death the sinner shall be converted; on the contrary,
He has often declared that he who lives in sin shall
die in sin: "You shall die in your sin." (*John* 8:21). He
has said that he who seeks Him at the hour of death
shall not find Him: "You shall seek me, and shall not
find me." (*John* 7:34). We must, then, seek God when
he can be found: "Seek ye the Lord while he may be
found." (*Isaias* 55:6). Yes; because a time will come
when He will not be found. Poor sinners! poor blind
ones! who wait to be converted till the hour of death,

when there will be no more time for conversion. "The wicked," says Oleaster, "will not learn to do evil or good till there is no more time for doing it." God wishes to save all, but He punishes the obstinate.

If perchance some unhappy sinner were to be seized with apoplexy, and deprived of his senses, what compassion would it not excite in all to see him dying without the sacraments, and without a sign of repentance! And what joy would everyone experience if he came to himself again, begged for absolution, and made acts of contrition! But is he not mad, who, having time to do this, continues in sin, or returns to sin, and runs the risk of being surprised by death, when he perhaps may, or perhaps may not, do it? It is terrible to see anyone die suddenly; and yet how many voluntarily incur the peril of dying thus, and of dying in sin!

"Weight and balance are judgments of the Lord." (*Prov.* 16:11). We keep no account of the graces God bestows on us; but the Lord keeps an account of them, and measures them; and when He sees them despised up to a certain point, He leaves the sinner in his sin, and in this state permits him to die. Miserable indeed is he who defers his repentance till death. "The repentance demanded of the sick is also of itself sickly," says St. Augustine.[11] St. Jerome says, "that out of a hundred thousand sinners who continue in sin till their death, scarcely one merits indulgence from God in death."[12] St. Vincent Ferrer says, "that it would be a greater miracle if habitual evil-livers had a good end than to raise the dead to life."[13] What sorrow, what repentance, can he conceive at the hour of death, who until then has loved sin? Bellarmine relates that having gone to assist a certain dying person, and having exhorted him to make an act of contrition, he replied that he did not know what contrition was. Bellarmine endeavored to explain it to him; but the sick man said: "Father, I do not understand you; I am not capable of these things." And thus he died, "leaving clear signs of his damnation," as is recorded in the writings of

Bellarmine. The just punishment of the sinner, says St. Augustine, will be, that having forgot God in his lifetime, he shall forget himself in death: "He is most justly struck, who having forgotten God in his lifetime, dies forgetful of himself."[14] "Be not deceived," says the Apostle, "God is not mocked: for what things a man shall sow, those also shall he reap. For he that soweth in his flesh, of the flesh also shall he reap corruption." (*Gal.* 6:7). It would be mocking God to live despising His laws, and then to receive a reward and eternal glory; but "God is not mocked." That which we sow in this life we shall reap in the next. He who sows the forbidden pleasures of the flesh shall reap nothing but corruption, misery, and eternal death.

Dear Christian, that which is said for others is said likewise for you. Tell me, if you were now at the point of death, given over by your physicians, deprived of your senses, and in your last agony, would you then not pray fervently to God to grant you another month, another week, to settle the accounts of your conscience? God gives you now this time. Return Him thanks, quickly repair the evil you have done, and take every means to restore yourself to a state of grace, and be so found when death comes; for then there will be no more time to remedy the past.

AFFECTIONS AND PRAYERS

Ah, my God, who would have had so much patience with me as Thou hast had! If Thy goodness were not infinite, I should despair of pardon. But I have to deal with a God who died to obtain my pardon and my salvation. Thou commandest me to hope, and I will hope. If my sins alarm and condemn me, Thy merits and Thy promises give me courage. Thou hast promised Thy grace to whoever returns to Thee: "Return ye, and live." (*Ezech.* 18:32). Thou hast promised to embrace whoever turns to Thee: "Turn ye to me, and I will turn to you." (*Zach.* 1:3). Thou hast said Thou canst not despise an humble and contrite heart. (*Psalms* 1). Behold me, Lord; I come again to Thee; I turn to Thee; I acknowledge that I deserve a thousand hells; and I repent of having offended Thee. I firmly promise never again to offend Thee, and always to love Thee. Ah, do not permit me to live any longer ungrateful to so much goodness. Eternal Father, through the merits of the obedience of Jesus Christ, who died to obey Thee, grant that I may obey Thy will until death. I love Thee, O my Sovereign Good; and through the love that I bear Thee, I will obey Thee in all things. Give me holy perseverance; give me Thy love, and I ask nothing more of Thee. Mary, my Mother, intercede for me.

CONSIDERATION VII

Sentiments of a Dying Negligent Christian, Who Has Thought Little of Death

> *"Take orders with thy house: for thou shalt die, and not live."*
>
> Isaias 38:1

FIRST POINT

Imagine yourself with a sick person who has only a few hours to live. Poor sufferer I behold how he is oppressed with pains, faintings, suffocation, want of breath, cold sweats, and weakness of head, to such a degree that he can hardly hear, understand, or speak. Amongst his miseries the greatest is, that death approaches, and instead of thinking of his soul, and preparing himself for eternity, he only thinks of physicians, and remedies to free him from the ailments and pains that are killing him. "They are unable to have any other thought than of themselves," says St. Laurence Justinian, speaking of such deaths. If, at least, his relations and friends forewarned the dying man of his danger; but no, there is not one amongst them all who has the courage to announce to him his approaching end, and to advise him to receive the last sacraments; everyone refuses to tell him for fear of vexing him. O my God, from this moment I thank Thee that in death Thou wilt cause me to be assisted by the dear brothers of my Congregation, who will then have no other interest but that of my eternal salvation, and will all aid me to die well.

But in the meantime, although no warning is given him of his death, the dying man nevertheless, seeing all the family in disorder, the frequent medical consultations, and the numberless and violent remedies that are adopted, is filled with confusion and terror, and amidst continual attacks of fear, remorse, and distrust, says within himself. "Alas, who knows but the end of my days is come!" What, then, will be his feelings when he really receives the announcement of his death! "Take order with thy house: for thou shalt die, and shalt not live." (*Isaias* 38:1). What distress when he hears these words! "Sir, your illness is mortal; you must receive the sacraments, make your peace with God, and bid farewell to the world." Bid farewell to the world? What! must I bid farewell to all? To that house, that villa, those relations, friends, conversations, games, amusements? Yes, to all. The lawyer is already come; and he writes this farewell: "I bequeath, I bequeath." And what does he carry with him? Nothing but a miserable rag, which will soon rot with him in the grave.

Oh, what sadness and perturbation will it cause to the dying man to perceive the tears of his servants, and the silence of his friends, who have not the courage to speak, in his presence! But the greatest of his pains will be the remorse of conscience, which will but make itself more clearly heard in that storm—for the disorderly life he has led up to that time, after so many calls and Divine lights, so many warnings from his spiritual fathers, and so many resolutions made, but either never performed or afterwards neglected. He will then say: Ah, unhappy that I am; I have had so many lights from God, so much time to settle my conscience, and I have not done it; and behold, now I have arrived at the hour of death! What would it have cost me to fly from that occasion, to detach myself from that friendship, to go to confession every week? And even if it had cost me much, I ought to have done all to save my soul, which was all-important. Oh, had I but performed that good resolution which I made; oh, had I continued as I then begun, how happy I should now be! But I have not done so; and now there is no time. The sentiments of such dying persons as have been careless during life of their conscience resembles those of the damned, who in Hell also lament over their sins as the cause of their pain, but without fruit and without remedy.

AFFECTIONS AND PRAYERS

O Lord, if, in this moment, the announcement of my approaching death were brought to me, such would be my sentiments of grief. I thank Thee for giving me this light, and time to amend. No, my God, I will no more fly from Thee. Thou hast sufficiently sought after me. I have just reason to fear that if I now resist, and do not return to Thee, Thou wilt abandon me. Thou hast given me a heart to love Thee, and I have made so bad a use of it; I have loved creatures, and I have not loved Thee, my Creator and my Redeemer, who hast given Thy life for me. Instead of loving Thee, how many times have I offended Thee, despised Thee, turned my back on Thee! I know that I displeased Thee by that sin, and yet I committed it. My Jesus, I repent of it, I am sorry for it with all my heart; I will change my life. I renounce all the pleasures of the world, that I may love and please Thee, O God of my soul. Thou hast given me great proofs of Thy love; would that I also could give Thee some proof of mine ere I die! From this moment I accept of all the illnesses, crosses, contempts, and annoyances, that I may receive from men; give me strength to suffer them in peace, for I will endure them all for the love of Thee. I love Thee O Infinite Goodness, I love Thee above every other good. Do Thou give me more love, and give me holy perseverance. Mary, my hope, pray to Jesus for me.

Second Point

Oh, how clearly at the moment of death are the truths of faith perceived! But for the greater torment of the dying man who has led a bad life, and especially if he has been a person consecrated to God, so that he has had more facilities for serving Him, more leisure, more good examples, more inspirations. O God, with what grief will he think and say: "I have admonished others, and yet I have done worse than they have; I quitted the world, and yet I have lived attached to pleasures, vanities, and the love of the world." With what remorse will he reflect, that with the lights he had received from God, even a pagan would have become a saint! With what pain will he recall having despised pious practices in others as proofs of weakness of mind; and having applauded certain worldly maxims of self-esteem, or self-love, such as not allowing others to take precedence of us, avoiding suffering, and seizing every opportunity of amusing ourselves!

"The desire of the wicked shall perish." (*Psalms* 111:9). How shall we covet in death that time which now we squander away! St. Gregory relates, in his dialogues, that a certain rich man of bad character, named Chrysantius, cried out when he was dying against the devils who visibly appeared to him to seize him: "Give me time, give me time, till tomorrow!" And these replied, "Thou fool, dost thou now ask for time? Thou hast had so much of it, and hast lost it, spending it in sin; and now dost thou ask for it? There is no more time now." The wretched man continued to call out, and to implore for help. A son of his, named Massimo, who was a monk, being with him, the dying man said, "My son, help me; my dear Massimo, help me!" And in the meanwhile, with his face all on fire, he flung himself furiously from one side of the bed to the other, and thus in agitation, and with cries of despair, he breathed forth his unhappy soul.

Alas, these madmen in life love their folly, but in death they open their eyes, and confess their folly; but then this only serves to increase their fears as to being able to repair the evil done; and dying thus, they leave great uncertainty as to their salvation. My brother, whilst you are reading this point, I imagine that you also say, "So it is." But if it is so, much greater would be your folly and misfortune, if knowing these truths in life, you did not amend in time. What you have now read will be a sword of sorrow for you in death.

Take courage, then, and since you have yet time to avoid so frightful a death, hasten to repair the past; do not wait for that time which will no longer be suitable for reparation. Do not wait for another month, nor another week. Who knows but this light, which God in His mercy now gives you, may be the last light, and the last call for you? It is folly not to think upon death, which is certain, and upon which an eternity depends; but it is still greater folly to think upon it, and not to prepare for it. Make now those reflections and resolutions which you would make then—now with profit, but then uselessly—now with confidence of being saved, then with great diffidence as to your salvation. A gentleman, who was about to take leave of the court of Charles V, that he might live only to God, being asked by the emperor why he left it, replied: "It is necessary, if we wish to be saved, that some period of penance should intervene between a life of disorder and death."

AFFECTIONS AND PRAYERS

No, my God, I will no more abuse Thy mercy. I thank Thee for the light Thou now givest me, and promise Thee to change my life. I see that Thou canst bear with me no longer. And shall I wait till Thou dost actually send me to Hell? or till Thou dost abandon me to a wicked life, which would be a greater punishment than death itself? Behold, I cast myself at Thy feet; receive me into Thy favor. I do not deserve it; but Thou hast said, "The wickedness of the wicked shall not hurt him, in whatsoever day he shall turn from his wickedness." (*Ezech.* 33:12). If, then, my Jesus, I have in past days offended Thy Infinite Goodness, I now repent of it with all my heart, and hope for Thy pardon. I will say to Thee, with St. Anselm, "Ah, do not permit that my soul should be lost through its sins, since Thou hast redeemed it with Thy Blood." Do not regard my ingratitude, but that love which caused Thee to die for me. If I have lost Thy grace, Thou hast not lost the power of restoring it to me. Have pity, then, upon me, O my dear Redeemer. Pardon me, and give me grace to love Thee; whilst from this day henceforth I promise to love Thee alone. Thou hast chosen me from amongst so many other possible creatures, to love Thee; I choose Thee, my Sovereign Good, to love Thee above every other good. Thou goest before me with Thy Cross; I will continually follow Thee with that cross which Thou givest me to carry. I embrace whatever mortifications and pains may come to me from Thee. As long as I am not deprived of Thy grace, I am content. Mary, my hope, obtain for me perseverance from God, and the grace to love Him, and I ask nothing more of thee.

THIRD POINT

The dying man who during his life has been careless as to the welfare of his soul, will find thorns in everything; thorns in the remembrance of past amusements, of rivalries overcome, and of pomp displayed; thorns in the friends who come to visit him, with all the recollections they bring with them; thorns in the spiritual fathers, who by turns will assist him; thorns in the sacraments of confession, communion, and extreme unction, which he must receive; a thorn likewise will that Crucifix become to him which will be placed before him, as he reads in that image how ill he has corresponded with the love of a God who died to save him.

"Oh, fool that I have been!" the poor sufferer will then say. "I might have become a saint, with all the lights and opportunities which God has given me; I might have led a life of happiness in the grace of God; and now what remains to me of the many years I have passed, but torments, distrusts, fears, remorse of conscience, and accounts to render to God? And hardly can I hope to save my soul." And when will he say this? When the oil of the lamp is nearly consumed, and the scene of this world is about to close; when he is already in sight of the two eternities, happy and unhappy; when he is near that last gasp, upon which depends his being in bliss or in despair for ever, as long as God is God. How much would he then give to have another year, or month, or at least another week of time, with the use of his senses; for laboring then under that distraction of head, oppression of the chest, and difficulty of breathing, he can do nothing; he cannot reflect, he cannot apply his mind to a single good act: he finds himself, as it were, enclosed in a dark pit of confusion, where he can conceive nothing but a great ruin impending over her, and which he is powerless to avert. Therefore would he wish for time; but it shall be said to him, "*Proficiscere,* depart; make haste, settle your accounts as you best can during this short space of time, and depart; do you not know that death neither waits for nor respects anyone?"

Oh, what a terror will it then be to him to think and say: "This morning I am alive; this evening most likely I shall be dead! Today I am in this room; tomorrow I shall be in the grave! And my soul, where will it be?" What terror when he sees the candle prepared! When he perceives the cold sweat of death appear! When he hears his relations ordered to withdraw from his room to return no more! When his sight begins to fail, and his eyes to darken! What terror, finally, when the candle is lighted, for death is already approaching! O candle, candle, how many truths will thy light then discover! Oh, how different wilt thou then show things to be from what they now appear! How clearly wilt thou show us that all the goods of this world are but vanity, folly, and deceits! But what will it avail us to understand these truths, when the time is past for profiting by them?

AFFECTIONS AND PRAYERS

Ah, my God, Thou desirest not my death, but that I should be converted and live. I thank Thee for having waited for me till now, and I thank Thee for the light Thou now givest me. I acknowledge the error I have committed in preferring to Thy friendship the vile and miserable pleasures for which I have despised Thee. I repent and grieve, with all my heart, for having done Thee so great a wrong. Ah, do not cease during the remainder of my life to assist me with Thy light and Thy grace to know and to do what I ought for my amendment. What will it avail me to know the truth, when the time for reparation is taken from me? "Deliver not up to beasts the souls that trust in Thee." When the devil shall tempt me to offend Thee again, ah, I beseech of Thee, my Jesus, through the merits of Thy passion, to stretch forth Thy hand and preserve me from falling into sin, and becoming again a slave to my enemies. Grant that I may then always have recourse to Thee, and never cease recommending myself to Thee as long as the temptation lasts. Thy Blood is my hope, and Thy goodness is my love. I love Thee, O my God, worthy of an infinite love; grant that I may always love Thee. Make me know from what things I must detach myself, that I may wholly belong to Thee, for this is my desire; but do Thou give me strength to execute it. O Queen of Heaven, O Mother of God, pray for me, a sinner; grant that, in all temptations I may ever have recourse to Jesus and to thee, who by thy intercession preservest those from falling who have recourse to thee.

CONSIDERATION VIII

The Death of the Just

"Precious in the sight of the Lord is the death of His saints."   Psalms 115:15

FIRST POINT

Death viewed according to the senses terrifies and causes fear; but when viewed with the eyes of faith it consoles and becomes desirable. It appears terrible to sinners, but lovely and precious to the saints. "Precious," says St. Bernard, "as the end of our labors, the consummation of victory, the gate of life."[15] Yes, death is the end of labor and toil. "Man born of a woman, living for a short time, is filled with many miseries." (*Job* 14:1). Such is our life, short, and full of miseries, infirmities, fears, and passions. "What," says Seneca, "do worldlings seek who desire a long life, but a prolonged torment?"[16] "What," says St. Augustine, "is a continuation of life but a continuation of suffering?"[17] Yes, because, as St. Ambrose tells us, our present life is not given us for repose, but for labor, and by labor to merit eternal life: "This life is not given to man for rest, but for labor." Hence Tertullian justly observes, that when God shortens the life of anyone, He shortens his pain: "God takes away

a long torment when He gives a short life." Hence,
although death was inflicted on man in punishment
of sin, yet notwithstanding, such are the miseries of
this life, as St. Ambrose observes, "that death would
appear to be given to us as a relief rather than a
chastisement." God calls those blessed who die in His
grace, because their labors are ended, and they go to
rest: "Blessed are the dead who die in the Lord. From
henceforth now, saith the Spirit, that they may rest
from their labours." (*Apoc.* 14:13).

The torments that afflict sinners at the hour of
death do not afflict the saints: "The souls of the just
are in the hands of God, and the torment of death
shall not touch them." (*Wis.* 3:1). The saints grieve not
when they hear that *Proficiscere,* which so terrifies
the worldly. The saints are not afflicted at leaving the
goods of this world, since they have kept their hearts
detached from them: "God of my heart," thus did they
unceasingly say, "and God is my portion in eternity."
Blessed are you, said the Apostle to his disciples, who
had been stripped of all their goods for Jesus Christ:
"You receive with joy the plundering of your goods,
knowing that you have a better and a permanent sub-
stance." (*Heb.* 10:34). They are not afflicted at leaving honors, because they had already detested them,
and regarded them, as they really are, but as smoke
and vanity; they esteemed only the honor of loving
and being loved by God. They are not afflicted at leaving their relations, because they have only loved them
in God; in dying they leave them under the care of
that heavenly Father who loves them more than they
do; and hoping to be saved, they think they can better assist them in Heaven than in this world. In fine,
that which they have always said in their lifetime,
"My God, and my all," they continue to repeat in death
with still greater consolation and tenderness.

He who dies loving God is not disturbed by the pains
that accompany death, but, on the contrary, he rather
feels complacency in them, reflecting that life is about

to end, and that no more time remains for him to suffer for God, and to give Him other proofs of his love; therefore, lovingly and peacefully he offers Him these last moments of his life, and consoles himself by uniting the sacrifice of his death with the sacrifice that Jesus Christ offered for him on the Cross to His eternal Father. And thus he happily expires, saying: "In him I will sleep, and repose in peace." (*Psalms* 4:8). Oh, what peace to die reposing in the arms of Jesus Christ, who has loved us even unto death, and has suffered a bitter, to obtain for us a sweet and consoling death!

AFFECTIONS AND PRAYERS

Ah, my beloved Jesus, who to obtain for me a happy death hast chosen to die so bitter a death on Calvary, when shall I behold Thee? The first time that I shall see Thee will be as my judge in the very place where I shall expire. What shall I then say to Thee? What wilt Thou say to me? I will not wait till that moment to think upon it, I will now anticipate it. I will say to Thee: My dear Redeemer, Thou then art He who died for me. At one time I offended Thee, and was ungrateful to Thee; I did not deserve Thy pardon: but afterwards, assisted by Thy grace, I entered into myself, and during the remainder of my life I wept for my sins, and Thou hast pardoned me. Pardon me again, now that I am at Thy feet, and give me Thyself a general absolution for my sins, I did not deserve to love Thee any more, since I had despised Thy love; but Thou in Thy mercy didst draw my heart to Thee; and if it has not loved Thee as Thou deservest, it has at least loved Thee above all things, leaving all to please Thee. Now, what sayest Thou to me? I know that Heaven and the possession of Thee in Thy kingdom is a blessing too great for me; but I dare not trust myself to live far from Thee, especially now that Thou hast shown me Thy amiable and beauteous face. I ask Heaven, then, of Thee, not that I may enjoy myself more, but

that I may love Thee more. Send me to purgatory for
as long as it may please Thee. No, I do not even desire
to enter into that land of purity, and to find myself
amongst those pure souls, defiled as I am at present
with stains. Send me to purify myself, but do not banish me for ever from Thy face; it is enough for me if
one day, in Thy own good time, Thou shouldst call me
to sing Thy mercies for all eternity in paradise. And
now, O my beloved Judge, come and raise Thy hand to
bless me, and tell me that I am Thine, and that Thou
art and wilt always be mine. I will always love Thee;
Thou wilt always love me. Behold, I go far from Thee,
I go into fire; but I go content, because I go to love
Thee, my Redeemer, my God, and my all. I go content;
yes, but know that, whilst I am far from Thee, this
absence from Thee will be the greatest of my pains I
go, O Lord, to count the moments till Thou callest me.
Have pity on a soul that loves Thee with all her powers, and sighs to behold Thee, that she may love Thee
better.

Thus, O my Jesus, I hope then to speak to Thee. In
the mean time I pray of Thee to give me the grace to
live in such a manner that I may then say to Thee
what I have now thought. Give me holy perseverance,
give me Thy love. And do thou assist me, O Mary,
Mother of God; pray to Jesus for me.

SECOND POINT

"God shall wipe away all tears from their eyes, and
death shall be no more." (*Apoc.* 21:4). The Lord, then,
in death shall wipe away from the eyes of His servants
the tears shed in this life, living, as they did, in pains,
fears, perils, and combats with Hell. The greatest consolation to a soul that has loved God, when death is
announced to her, will be the thought that she will
soon be delivered from the many dangers there are in
this life of offending God, the many troubles of conscience, and the many temptations of the devil. The

present life is a continual war with Hell, in which we are in constant danger of losing our Lord and God. St. Ambrose says, that in this world "we walk always amidst the snares of enemies," who lie in wait to rob us of the life of grace. This danger caused St. Peter of Alcantara to say, when he was dying, to a religious who in assisting him touched him: "My brother, keep away from me, because I am still living, and in peril of being damned." This danger likewise caused St. Teresa to be comforted each time that she heard the clock strike, rejoicing that another hour of combat had passed, for she said, "In every moment of life I may sin and lose God." Hence the Saints are full of consolation when death is announced to them, reflecting that their battles and perils are at an end, and that they will soon be secure of that happy state when they can never more lose God.

It is related in the lives of the Fathers, that an aged Father dying in Scythia, laughed whilst the others wept. Being asked why he laughed, he replied: "And you, why do you weep, seeing that I go to rest? I pass from labor to rest, and do you weep?" So also St Catherine of Sienna when dying, said: "Rejoice with me, for I quit the land of sorrows, and go to a place of peace." "If anyone," says St. Cyprian, "were to inhabit a house whose walls were falling, and whose floors and roofs trembled, so that all threatened destruction, how much would he desire to get out of it!" In this life everything threatens ruin to the soul; the world, Hell, the passions, the rebellious senses, all draw us on to sin and to everlasting death. "Who shall deliver me," says the Apostle, "from the body of this death?" (*Rom.* 7:24). Oh, how great will be the joy of the soul when it hears these words: "Come from Libanus, my spouse; come from the dens of lions." (*Cant.* 4:8). Come, my spouse, depart from the land of tears and from the dens of lions, who seek to devour thee, and to make thee lose Divine grace. Hence St. Paul, sighing for death, said that Jesus Christ was his only life: and therefore he regarded death as his greatest gain, because by death he obtained that life which never ends: "For to me to live is Christ, and to die is gain." (*Phil.* 1:21).

God confers a great favor on a soul that is in the state of grace when He takes her from this world, where she may change and lose His friendship. "He was taken away, lest wickedness should alter his understanding." (*Wis.* 4:7). Happy he who in this life lives united to God; but as the sailor cannot be called secure till has entered the port and escaped the storm, so a soul cannot be called completely happy till she has quitted this life in the grace of God. "Praise the good fortune of the sailor," says St. Ambrose; "but not till he has entered the port." Now if the gained rejoices when, after so many dangers, he has nearly gained the port, how much more must he rejoice who is on the point of securing eternal salvation!

Moreover, in this life it is impossible to live without sin, at least venial: "The just man shall fall seven times." (*Prov.* 24:16). He who leaves this life ceases to offend God. "What is death," says St. Ambrose, "but the sepulchre of sin?"[19] This also it is that causes those who love God to be so desirous of death. This filled the venerable Father Vincent Caraffa with consolation at the hour of death; so that he said, "In ceasing to live, I cease to offend God." St. Ambrose, also: "Why do we desire this life, in which the longer we remain the more we are laden with sins?" He who dies in the grace of God is placed in a state in which he neither is able nor knows how to offend God any more. "The dead cannot sin," says the same Saint. Therefore does the Lord praise the dead more than any living man, although he be a saint: "I praised the dead rather than the living." (*Ecclus.* 4:2). A certain virtuous man commanded that whoever should have to announce his death to him should say to him, "Be comforted, for the time is come when thou shalt no longer offend God."

AFFECTIONS AND PRAYERS

"Into Thy hands I commend my spirit; Thou hast redeemed me, O Lord, the God of truth." Ah, my sweet Redeemer, what would have become of me, had I died whilst I dwelt far from Thee, I should now be in Hell, where I could never love Thee more. I thank Thee for not having abandoned me, and for having bestowed on me so many graces to win my heart to Thee. I repent of having offended Thee. I love Thee above all things. Ah, I implore of Thee to make me more and more sensible of the evil I have committed in despising Thee, and of the love which Thy infinite goodness deserves. I love Thee, and I desire to die speedily, if such be Thy will, that I may be delivered from the danger of again losing Thy holy grace, and be secure of loving Thee for ever. Ah, my beloved Jesus, during the remaining years of my life, give me strength to do something for Thee, ere death comes upon me. Give me strength against my temptations and passions, especially against that passion which in the past has most caused me to displease Thee. Give me patience under infirmities, and under the injuries that I may receive from men, I now pardon, for the love of Thee, all who have shown me any contempt, and I beseech Thee to grant them the graces they desire. Give me strength to be more diligent in avoiding even venial sins, in regard of which I know myself to be careless. My Saviour, help me; I hope for all through Thy merits; and I confide all to thy intercession, O Mary, my Mother, and my hope.

THIRD POINT

"Death is not only the end of labors, but it is also the gate of life," says St. Bernard. He who wishes to see God must necessarily pass through this gate: "This is the gate of the Lord; the just shall enter into it." (*Psalms* 117:20). St. Jerome called upon death, and said, "Open to me, my sister." Death, my sister, if thou dost not open the gate, I cannot go to enjoy my Lord. St. Charles Borromeo, seeing a picture in his house which represented a skeleton with a scythe in its hand, sent for the painter, and ordered him to erase the scythe, and to paint a golden key, that thus he might he more and more inflamed with the desire of death, since it is death that admits us into Heaven to behold God.

If a king, says St. John Chrysostom, had prepared apartments for some one in his palace, but for the present obliged him to inhabit a hovel, how much would this person desire to leave the hovel and go to the palace! The soul in this life being in the body is as it were in a prison, which she must leave to enter the kingdom of Heaven; therefore David prayed: "Take my soul out of prison." (*Psalms* 141:10). And the holy Simeon, when he held the Infant Jesus in his arms, asked for no favor but death, that he might be delivered from the prison of the present life: "Now thou dost dismiss thy servant, O Lord." (*Luke* 2:29). St. Ambrose observes: "He begs to be dismissed, as if he were detained by necessity." The Apostle desired the same favor when he said, "I desire to be dissolved, and to be with Christ." (*Phil.* 1:23).

How great was the joy of Pharao's cup-bearer when he heard from Joseph that he should soon leave his prison, and return to his post! And shall a soul that loves God not rejoice to hear that she will shortly be liberated from this earth, and go to enjoy God? "While we are in the body, we, are absent from the Lord." (*2 Cor.* 5:6). As long as we are united to the body, we are at a distance from the sight of God, in a strange land, and excluded from our own country: "and therefore," says St. Bruno, "our death ought not to be called death, but the beginning of life." Hence the death of the saints is called their nativity; yes, because in their death they are born to that blessed life which shall have no end. St. Athanasius says, "The just do not die, but are translated." Death to the just is only a passage to eternal life. "O amiable death," said St. Augustine, "who is he that desires thee not, since thou art the termination of troubles, the end of labor, the beginning of eternal repose?" Hence the saint earnestly prayed: "May I die, O Lord, that I may see Thee!"

Well may the sinner fear death, says St. Cyprian, who From temporal death will pass into eternal death: "Let him fear to die, who shall pass from this death to the second death;" but not he, who being in the grace of God, will pass from death to life. In the life of St. John the Almoner it is related, that a certain rich man recommended his only son to the prayers of the Saint, and gave him great alms, that he might obtain a long life for him of God; but he died soon after. As the father was lamenting over the death of his son, God sent to him an angel, who said: "Thou hast sought a long life for thy son; know that he already enjoys it eternally in Heaven." This is the grace that Jesus Christ obtained for us, as was promised by Osee: "O Death, I shall be thy death." (Osee 13:14). Jesus, in dying for us, caused our death to become life. When Pionius the martyr was taken to execution, he was asked by those who conducted him, how he could go thus joyfully to death. The Saint replied, "You deceive yourselves; I do not go to death, but to life."[20] Thus also the youthful St. Symphorian was encouraged by his mother, when the time of his martyrdom approached: "O my son, life is not taken from thee, but changed into a better."

AFFECTIONS AND PRAYERS

O God of my soul, I have hitherto dishonored Thee by turning my back on Thee; but Thy Son has honored Thee by sacrificing His life to Thee on the Cross. Through the honor, then, rendered Thee by Thy beloved Son, pardon me for having dishonored Thee, I repent, O my Sovereign Good, of having offended Thee, and I promise from this day henceforth to love only Thee. From Thee

I hope for my salvation. Whatever at present I possess
of good is through Thy mercy and grace; I acknowledge
it to be all from Thee: "By the grace of God, I am what
I am." If in the past I have dishonored Thee, I hope to
honor Thee in eternity, in blessing Thy mercy. I feel in
myself a great desire to love Thee: this is Thy gift; I
thank Thee for it, O my Love. Continue, oh, continue
to help me as Thou hast begun; and I hope from this
day henceforth to be Thine, and wholly Thine. I renounce
all the pleasures of the world. And what greater pleasure can I have than to please Thee, my most amiable
Lord, who hast loved me so much I ask only for love,
O my God—love, love—and I hope always to ask of
Thee love, love; until dying in Thy love, I attain to the
kingdom of love, where, without asking any more for
it, I shall be full of love, and never cease for one moment
to love Thee during all eternity with all my strength,
Mary, my Mother, thou who so much lovest thy God,
and so much desirest to see Him loved, grant that I
may love Him much in this life, in order that I may
love Him much in the next forever.

CONSIDERATION IX

Peace of the Just at the Hour of Death

> *"The souls of the just are in the hands*
> *of God, and the torment of death shall not*
> *touch them. In the sight of the unwise they*
> *seemed to die; . . . but they are in peace."*
> Wisdom 3:1

FIRST POINT

"The souls of the just are in the hands of God." If
God holds the souls of the just fast in His hands, who
can snatch them from Him? It is true that Hell ceases
not to tempt and to insult even the saints at the time

of their death; but God ceases not to assist them, and, as St. Ambrose observes, to increase His aids to His faithful servants as their perils increase: "There is greater aid where there is greater danger; for God is our helper in the time of need."[21] When the servant of Eliseus saw the city surrounded by enemies, he was terrified; but the saint encouraged her, saying: "Fear not, for there are more with us than with them." (*4 Kings* 6:16). And he then showed him an army of angels sent by God to defend the city. The devil indeed will come to tempt the dying man, but his guardian angel will also come to comfort him; the saints, his holy advocates, will come; St. Michael, who is appointed by God to defend His faithful servants in their last combat with Hell, will come. Our holy Mother will come to chase away all enemies by placing her servant under the mantle of her protection. Above all, Jesus Christ will come to guard against temptations His innocent or penitent sheep, for whose salvation He has given His life. He will give that confidence and strength of which the soul stands in need in such a struggle, so that full of courage she will say, "The Lord became my helper." (*Psalms* 29:10). "The Lord is my light and my salvation; whom shall I fear?" (*Psalms* 26:1). God, says Origen, is more solicitous for our salvation than the devil for our perdition; for God loves us far more than the devil hates us: "He has greater care to lead us to salvation than the devil to drive us to damnation."[22]

God is faithful, says the Apostle; He does not permit us to be tempted above our strength: "Who will not suffer you to be tempted above that which you are able." (*1 Cor.* 10:13). But you will say: Many saints have died in great fear for their salvation. I reply, that we read of but few examples of those who, having led a good life, have died in this fear. Belluacensis says, that the Lord permits it in some, to purify them in death from some defect: "The just are sometimes purified in this world by a severe struggle at the time of death." However, we read of almost all the servants of

God, that they died with a smile on their lips. The judgments of God excite fear in all; but where sinners pass from fear to despair, the saints pass from fear to confidence. St. Antoninus relates that St. Bernard being ill, was afraid, and tempted to want of confidence; but reflecting upon the merits of Jesus Christ, he banished all fear, saying, "Thy wounds are my merits." St. Hilarion feared, but he afterwards joyously said, "Go forth, my soul; of what art thou afraid? For near seventy years thou hast served Christ, and dost thou now fear death?" As if he had said: My soul, what dost thou fear, having served a God who is faithful, and who never forsakes those who have been faithful to Him in life? Father Joseph Scamacca, of the Society of Jesus, being asked whether he died with confidence, replied: "What! have I served Mahomet, that I should now doubt of the goodness of my God, that He will not save me?"

If we should happen in death to be tormented by the thought of having at some period offended God, we know that the Lord has declared He will forget the sins of the penitent: "If the wicked do penance for all the sins he hath committed, I will not remember all his iniquities." (*Ezech.* 18:21). But, it may be said, how can we be sure that God has pardoned us? St. Basil asks the same question, and replies: "Provided we can say, I hate and abominate my iniquities."[23] He who hates sin may be sure that God has pardoned him. The heart of man cannot exist without love: it either loves creatures, or it loves God; if it does not love creatures, then it loves God. And who loves God? He who observes His commandments: "He that hath my commandments and keepeth them, he it is that loveth me." (*John* 14:21). He, then, who dies in the observance of His commandments, dies loving God; and he who loves God fears not. "Charity casteth out fear." (*1 John* 4:8).

AFFECTIONS AND PRAYERS

Ah, my Jesus, when will that day come in which I can say to Thee: My God, I can never lose Thee more? That day when I shall behold Thee face to face, and be secure of loving Thee with all my strength for all eternity? Ah, my Sovereign Good, my only Love, as long as I live I shall always be in danger of offending Thee, and of losing Thy lovely grace. There was an unhappy time when I loved Thee not and when I despised Thy love: now I repent with all my soul, and I hope Thou hast already pardoned me; and now I love Thee with all my heart, and I desire to do all I can to love and please Thee. But I am still in danger of refusing Thee my love, and of again turning my back on Thee. Ah, my Jesus, my Life, my Treasure, do not permit it. Rather than allow this greatest of misfortunes to befall me, let me die this moment the most cruel death it may please Thee to send me: I am content, and I pray for it. Eternal Father, for the love of Jesus Christ, do not abandon me to this utter ruin. Chastise me as Thou wilt; I deserve it, and I accept of it: but deliver me from the punishment of being deprived of Thy grace and Thy love. My Jesus, recommend me to Thy Father. Mary, my Mother, recommend me to thy Son; obtain for me perseverance in His friendship, and the grace of loving Him, and then may He do with me according to His will.

SECOND POINT

"The souls of the just are in the hands of God, and the torment of death shall not touch them. In the sight of the unwise they seemed to die . . . but they are in peace." (*Wis.* 3:1). In the sight of the unwise the servants of God seem to die afflicted and reluctantly, as worldlings do; but no, God well knows how to comfort His children in death; and even amidst the pains of death He makes them feel a certain incomparable

sweetness, as a foretaste of that paradise which He is about to bestow on them. As those who die in sin begin on their deathbed to experience certain fore-tastes of Hell—remorse, terrors, and despair—so, on the other hand, the saints—by acts of the love of God, which they then more frequently make, by the desire and the hope they possess of soon enjoying Him—begin even before death to experience that peace which they will afterwards fully enjoy in Heaven. To them death is not a punishment, but a reward: "When he shall give sleep to his beloved: behold the inheritance of the Lord." (*Psalms* 126:4). The death of him who loved God is not called death, but sleep; so that he can truly say, "In peace in the selfsame I will sleep, and I will rest." (*Psalms* 4:8). Father Suarez died in such peace, that at the moment of death he was able even to say: "I could never have imagined that death would be to me so sweet." Cardinal Baronius, being advised by his physician not to think so much upon death, replied: "And why? Is it that perchance I fear it? I do not fear it, but I love it." When Cardinal Fisher, Bishop of Rochester, was going to die for the faith, he dressed himself in the best clothes he had, saying, as is related by Saunders, that he was going to a wedding. When he came in sight of the scaffold he threw away his staff, and said: "My feet, make haste, for we are not far from paradise." Before be died, be intoned the *Te Deum,* in thanksgiving to God for permitting him to die a martyr for the holy faith; and thus full of joy he bent his head under the axe. St. Francis of Assisi sung when he was dying, and invited the oth-ers to sing. "Father," said brother Elias, "we ought to weep, and not to sing when we die." "But I cannot help singing," replied the saint, "when I reflect that I shall so soon go to enjoy God." A Teresian nun, who died young, said to the other nuns, who were weep-ing round her: "O God, why do you weep? I go to find my Jesus: rejoice with me, if you love me."[24]
Father Granada relates, that a certain huntsman

found a solitary leper singing whilst he was dying. "How," said he, "canst thou sing in such a state?" The hermit replied, "Brother, between me and God there is only the wall of this my body; I now see it falling to pieces, the prison is about to be destroyed, and I see God; therefore do I rejoice and sing." This desire to see God caused St. Ignatius the martyr to say, that if the wild beasts took not his life, he would provoke them to devour him. St. Catherine of Genoa could not endure that anyone should consider death as a misfortune, and she said: "O beloved death, in what a false light art thou viewed! Why, then, dost thou not co me to me, who call upon thee day and night?"[25] St. Teresa so much desired death, that she considered it death not to die; and in these sentiments she composed her celebrated hymn, "I die, because I do not die." Such is death to the Saints.

AFFECTIONS AND PRAYERS

Ah, my Sovereign Good, my God, if in time I have not loved Thee, I now turn myself wholly to Thee. I bid farewell to all creatures, and I choose to love only Thee, my most amiable Lord. Tell me what Thou desirest of me, and I will do it. I have offended Thee enough. I will spend all the remainder of my life in pleasing Thee. Give me strength that I may atone by my love for the ingratitude I have hitherto shown Thee. I have deserved for so many years to be burning in the fire of Hell, and Thou hast sought after me till Thou hast drawn me to Thyself; grant that I may now burn with the fire of Thy holy love, I love Thee, O Infinite Goodness. Thou desirest that I should love Thee alone; and with reason, for Thou hast loved me above all, and Thou alone deservest to be loved, and I will love only Thee; I will do all that I can to please Thee. Do with me what Thou wilt. It is enough for me that I love Thee, and that Thou lovest me. Mary, my Mother, assist me; pray to Jesus for me.

THIRD POINT

And how can he fear death, says St. Cyprian, who hopes after death to be crowned in Heaven: "Let us not be afraid to be put to death, of whom it is certain that we shall be crowned after death." How can he fear to die who knows that by dying in a state of grace his body will become immortal? "This mortal must put on immortality." (*1 Cor.* 15:53). He who loves God and desires to see Him regards life as a punishment, says St. Augustine, and death as a delight: "He lives with patience, he dies with delight." And St. Thomas of Villanova says, that if death find a man sleeping, it comes like a thief, robs him, kills him, and casts him into the pit of Hell; but if it find him watching, as the ambassador of God, it salutes him, and says: "The Lord expects thee at the nuptial feast; come, and I will conduct thee to the blessed kingdom thou desirest: The Lord calls thee to the marriage; come, I will lead thee where thou desirest."

Oh, with what joy does he await death who is in the grace of God, hoping soon to see Jesus Christ, and to hear these words, "Well done, good and faithful servant; because thou hast been faithful over a few things, I will place thee over many!" (*Matt.* 15:21). Oh, how will the value of penance, prayer, detachment from worldly goods, and all that has been done for God, then be known! "Say to the just man: It is well; for he shall eat the fruit of his doings." (*Isaias* 3:10). Then will he who has loved God taste the fruit of all his holy works. Therefore did Father Hippolitus Durazzo, of the Society of Jesus, rejoice instead of weep when a friend of his, a religious, died with every sign of salvation. But how absurd, said St. John Chrysostom, would it be to believe in an eternal Heaven, and yet to compassionate those who go to it: "To believe in Heaven, and to weep over those who go hence to it."[26] What a special consolation will it then be to remember the honors paid to the Mother of God, the rosaries recited, the visits to her altars, the fasts on Saturdays, the having frequented her confraternities! Mary is called Virgin most faithful; oh, how great is her fidelity in consoling her faithful servants at the hour of death! A certain person, devoted to the Blessed Virgin, said, in dying, to the Father Binetti: "Father, you cannot conceive what a consolation at the hour of death is the thought of having served our Blessed Lady. Oh, my Father, if you could but know what happiness I experience in having served this dear Mother! I know not how to express it." How great will be the joy of him who has loved Jesus Christ, who has often visited Him in the Blessed Sacrament, and who has often received Him in the Holy Communion, when he beholds his Lord enter his room in the Most Holy Viaticum, to accompany him in his passage to the next world! Happy he who can say to Him then, with St. Philip Neri, "Behold my love, behold my love; give me my love."

But some will say: Who can tell what my fate will be? Who knows but, after all, I shall make an unhappy end? But I ask of you who speak thus: What is it that renders death unhappy? Sin only; sin only, then, need we fear, and not death, "It is clear," says St. Ambrose, "that it is not death that is bitter, but sin: our fears ought not to be of death, but of life."[27] Do you desire, then, not to fear death? Live well. "With him that feareth the Lord, it shall go well in the latter end."

Father Colombière held it to be morally impossible that one who has been faithful to God during life should make a bad or an unhappy end. And St. Augustine before him had said: "He cannot die badly who has lived well." He who is prepared to die fears not any death, even though it be sudden. "But the just man, if he be prevented with death, shall be in rest." (*Wis.* 4:7). And since we cannot enjoy God except by death, St. John Chrysostom thus exhorts us: "Let us offer to God that which we are obliged to give Him." And let us be assured that he who offers his death to God makes the most perfect act of love of which he

is capable towards Him; since by willingly embracing
that death which it pleases God to send him, and in
that time and manner which God wills, he imitates
the holy martyrs. He who loves God must desire and
sigh for death, because death unites us eternally to
God, and delivers us from the danger of losing Him.
It is a sign of little love for God not to desire to go
quickly to see Him, with the certainty of never again
being able to lose Him. In the meantime let us love
Him as much as we can in this life. We should make
use of life only to advance in Divine love. The degree
of love in which death will find us will be the measure of our love for God in a happy eternity.

AFFECTIONS AND PRAYERS

Bind me, O my Jesus, to Thee, so that I can never
more be separated from Thee. Grant that I may belong
wholly to Thee ere I die; so that when I first behold
Thee, O my Redeemer, I may behold Thee appeased.
Thou soughtest me when I fled from Thee. Ah, do not
drive me from Thee now that I seek Thee. Pardon me
all the displeasure I have given Thee. From this day
henceforth I will think only of serving and loving Thee.
My obligations to Thee are too great. Thou hast not
refused to give Thy blood and Thy life for the love of
me. I should therefore wish to be wholly consumed for
Thee, O my Jesus, as Thou wert wholly consumed for
me. O God of my soul, I wish to love Thee much in
this life, that I may love Thee much in the next. Eternal Father, ah, draw my whole heart to Thee; detach
it from earthly affections, wound it, inflame it with
Thy holy love. Hear me, through the merits of Jesus
Christ. Give me holy perseverance; and give me the
grace to ask it always of Thee. Mary, my Mother, assist
me, and obtain for me this grace; to ask unceasingly
of thy Son holy perseverance.

CONSIDERATION X

Means of Preparing for Death

*"Remember thy last end, and thou shalt
never sin."*   Ecclesiasticus 7:40

FIRST POINT

All acknowledge that they must die, and die but
once; and that there is nothing of higher importance
than this, since on the moment of death depends our
eternal happiness or eternal despair. All know, moreover, that this death will be good or evil, according as
they have lived well or ill. And yet how is it that the
greater part of Christians live as if they were never
to die, or as if it signified little whether they died ill
or well? Our life is evil, because we think not of death:
"Remember thy last end, and thou shalt never sin."
We must be persuaded that the time of death is not
the time for settling our accounts, in order to secure
the great affair of our eternal salvation. In temporal
affairs the prudent ones of the world take in due time
all the measures for obtaining that gain, that post of
honor, that marriage; and as for the health of the body,
they defer not a moment applying the necessary remedies. What would you say of a man who, having under-
taken an academical contest, deferred preparing himself
for it till the time was come? Would not that general
be thought mad who deferred laying in stores of provi-
sions and arms till he were besieged? That pilot insane
who neglected to provide himself with anchors and
cables till overtaken by the storm? Such precisely is
the Christian who waits to settle the affairs of his conscience till death is actually at his door: "When sudden calamity shall fall on you then shall they call upon
me, and I will not hear: they shall eat the fruit of their
own way." (*Prov.* 1:27, 31). The time of death is the
time of storm and confusion; then sinners call upon

God to help them, but only from the fear of Hell, to
which they find themselves near, and without any true
conversion of the heart; and therefore God hears them
not: "Man shall reap what he has sown." Ah, it will
not then be sufficient to receive the Sacraments: we
must die detesting sin, and loving God above all things.
But how can he detest forbidden pleasures who till
then has loved them? How can he then love God above
all things, who until that moment has loved creatures
more than God? Those virgins were truly called foolish by our Lord who delayed preparing their lamps till
the Bridegroom was at hand. We all fear sudden death,
because there is no time then to settle our accounts.
All acknowledge that the saints have been truly wise,
because they prepared for death before it arrived. And
what do we do? Shall we expose ourselves to the risk
of having to prepare for dying well when death is close
upon us? We must do now that which we shall wish
to have done when we come to die. Oh, how grievous
to us then will be the remembrance of time lost, and
still more of time ill spent! time given to us by God
for meriting, but time past to return no more. With
what anguish shall we then hear: "Thou canst be no
longer steward!" There is no more time for doing
penance, for frequenting the Sacraments, for hearing
sermons, for visiting Jesus Christ in the churches, for
prayers. What is done is done. We need, then, a mind
more sound, a time more quiet to make our confession
as it ought to be made, to resolve various points of
serious scruple, and thus to tranquilize our conscience;
but "there will be no more time."

AFFECTIONS AND PRAYERS

Ah, my God, had I died in one of those nights Thou
knowest of, where should I now be? I thank Thee for
having waited for me; and I thank Thee for all those
moments which I should have spent in Hell, from that
first instant when I offended Thee. Ah, give me light,

and grant me to know the great wrong I have done Thee in voluntarily losing Thy grace, which Thou hast merited for me, by sacrificing Thyself for me on a cross. Ah, my Jesus, pardon me, for I grieve with all my heart, and above every evil, for having despised Thy infinite goodness, and I hope Thou hast already pardoned me. Assist me, O my Saviour, that I may never lose Thee more. Ah, my Lord, if I should again offend Thee, after having received so many lights and so many graces from Thee, should I not deserve a hell made expressly for me? By the merits of that Blood which Thou hast shed for the love of me, do not permit it. Give me holy perseverance; give me Thy love. I love Thee, my Sovereign Good; and I will never cease to love Thee till I die. My God, have pity on me, for the love of Jesus Christ. And thou also, Mary, my hope, have pity on me, recommend me to God; thy recommendations are never rejected by that Lord who so much loves thee.

SECOND POINT

My brother, since it is certain you must die, quickly cast yourself at the feet of your crucified Redeemer; thank Him for the time He gives you in His mercy to settle the affairs of your conscience, and then review all the disorders of your past life, especially those of your youth. Glance over the Divine precepts, examine your occupations, the society you have frequented, mark down in writing your failings, make a general confession of all your life, if you have not already done so. Oh, how useful is a good general confession for regulating the life of a Christian! Reflect that these are accounts for eternity; and therefore settle them as if you were about to render them to Jesus Christ your Judge. Banish from your heart every evil affection, every rancorous feeling; remove every ground of scruple regarding the property of others, characters destroyed, scandals given, and resolve to fly those occasions in

which you may lose God. Reflect that what now appears
difficult, at the moment of death will appear to you
impossible.

That which is of most importance is, to resolve to
practice the means for preserving yourself in the grace
of God. These means are, mass every day, meditations
upon the eternal truths, frequenting confession and
communion at least every eight days, a visit every day
to the Most Holy Sacrament and to the Divine Mother,
to belong to a confraternity, spiritual reading, examination of conscience every evening, some special devotion to our Blessed Lady—such as fasting on the
Saturday—and above all propose to recommend yourself often to God and to the Blessed Virgin, invoking
frequently, and especially in time of temptation, the
most holy names of Jesus and Mary: these are the
means by which you can obtain a happy death and
eternal salvation.

The practice of these will be a great mark of your
predestination. And as for the past, trust in the Blood
of Jesus Christ, who now gives you these lights because
He wishes to save you; and confide in the intercession
of Mary, who obtains these lights for you. With such
a rule of life, and confidence in Jesus and Mary, oh,
how does God aid us, and what strength does the soul
acquire! Quickly, then, dear reader, give yourself wholly
to God, who calls you, and begin to enjoy that peace,
of which you have hitherto been deprived through your
fault. And what greater peace can a soul feel than in
being able to say on lying down at night: Should death
come this night, I hope to die in the grace of God.
What a consolation is it to hear the thunder roll, to
feel the earth tremble, and to await death with resignation, if God so ordain it!

AFFECTIONS AND PRAYERS

Ah, my Lord, how much do I thank Thee for the light
Thou hast given me! I have so often left Thee, I have

turned my back upon Thee; but Thou hast not forsaken me. If Thou hadst abandoned me, I should have remained blind, as I have hitherto chosen to be; I should have been obstinate in my sin, and I should neither have had the will to forsake it nor the will to love Thee. Now I feel a great sorrow for having offended Thee, and a great desire to be in Thy grace: I abhor those accursed pleasures which have caused me to lose Thy friendship: all these are graces which come from Thee, and make me hope that Thou wilt pardon and save me. Since, then, with all my many sins, Thou hast not abandoned me, and desirest to save me, behold, Lord, I give myself wholly to Thee; I grieve for having offended Thee above every evil; and I resolve to lose my life a thousand times rather than Thy grace. I love Thee, my Sovereign Good; I love Thee, my Jesus, who hast died for me; and I hope in Thy Blood that Thou wilt not permit me ever again to be separated from Thee. No, my Jesus, I will never lose Thee more. I will love Thee always in life; I will love Thee in death; I will love Thee for all eternity. Preserve me, then, always, and increase in me my love for Thee, I ask it through Thy merits. Mary, my hope, pray to Jesus for me.

THIRD POINT

We must endeavor, moreover, to be at all times such as we desire to be found at the hour of death: "Blessed are the dead who die in the Lord." (*Apoc.* 14:13). St. Ambrose says that those die well who at the time of death are already dead to the world, that is, detached from those goods from which death will then forcibly separate us. So that we must from this moment accept of the loss of our property, the separation from our relations and from all the things of this earth. Unless we do this willingly in life, we shall have to do it of necessity in death; but then with great sorrow, and with peril to our eternal salvation. Therefore does St. Augustine admonish us that, in order to die in peace,

it behooves us to settle our temporal interests during
life, making now the proper disposition of the property we have to leave; so that in death we may be
solely occupied in uniting ourselves to God. Our dis-
course ought then to be of God and Heaven alone. Too
precious are those last moments to be wasted in
thoughts of earth. The crown of the elect is perfected
in death, since it is then, perhaps, that we reap the
greatest harvest of merits, by embracing those pains
and that death with resignation and love.

But he cannot have these good sentiments in death
who has not exercised them during life. Therefore some
devout persons, with great profit to themselves, are
accustomed to renew every month, after confession and
communion, the protestation for death, with the Christian acts, imagining themselves to be on their deathbed and about to quit this life. (This protestation and
the acts are contained in our little book of Visits to
the Blessed Sacrament; and being brief, can soon be
read.*) That which is not done in life is very difficult
to be done in death. That great servant of God, Sister
Catherine of St. Albert, a Teresian, when she was dying,
sighed, and said: My sisters, I do not sigh through the
fear of death, because for twenty-five years I have been
expecting it; I sigh to see so many deceive themselves,
by leading a life of sin, and reduced to make their
peace with God at the moment of death, in which I
am hardly able to pronounce the name of Jesus.

Examine, then, my brother, if your heart be now attached to any thing on this earth—to that person, to
that honor, to that house, that money, those conversations, those amusements; and remember that you
are not immortal. You will have to leave all one day,
and that perhaps soon. Why, then, cherish an attachment to them, and run the risk of an unquiet death?
Offer up all from this moment to God; be ready to give
up everything whenever it shall please Him. If you
desire to die resigned, you must from this time resign

* In the present edition it is in the volume on the *Christian Virtues*, p. 369.—Editor

yourself to all the adverse events that may befall you, and divest yourself of all affection to earthly things. Place before your eyes the moment of death, and despise all. "He," says St. Jerome, "easily despises all things who continually remembers that he must die."

If you have not yet decided upon a state of life, choose that state which you would wish to have chosen when you are expiring, and which will give you most satisfaction in dying. If, however, you have already made your election, do what you would then wish you had done in that state. Act as if every day were to be the last of your life, and every action the last; every prayer, every confession, every communion the last. Imagine yourself every hour as if you were expiring, stretched on a bed, and hearing that last intimation: "Depart from this world." Oh, how will this thought aid you to walk well through this world and detach you from it: "Blessed is that servant, whom when his Lord shall come, he shall find so doing." (*Matt.* 24:46). He who expects death every hour will die well even though he die suddenly.

AFFECTIONS AND PRAYERS

Every Christian ought to be prepared to say in that moment when death shall be announced to him: So, then, my God, but a few hours remain for me. I will, during these few hours, love Thee as much as I can in this life, that I may love Thee more in the next. But little is left for me to offer Thee; I offer Thee these pains and the sacrifice of my life in union with the sacrifice that Jesus Christ made for me on the Cross. O Lord, the pains that I endure are few and light compared with what I have deserved. Such as they are, I embrace them in token of the love I bear Thee. I resign myself to all the chastisements it may please Thee to inflict upon me in this and in the other life: provided that I love Thee in eternity, punish me as Thou wilt, but do not deprive me of Thy love. I know that I do not deserve to love Thee, since I have so often despised Thy love; but Thou canst not reject a penitent soul. I am sorry, O my Sovereign Good, for having offended Thee. I love Thee with all my heart, and place all my trust in Thee. Thy death, my Redeemer, is my hope. Into Thy wounded hands I commend my spirit. O my Jesus, Thou hast given Thy Blood to save me; do not suffer me to be separated from Thee. I love Thee, O eternal God; and I hope to love Thee in eternity, Mary, my Mother, assist me at the awful moment of my death. I now commend my spirit to thee; tell thy Son to have pity on me. I recommend myself to thee; oh, deliver me from Hell.

CONSIDERATION XI

On the Unhappy Life of the Sinner, and the Happy Life of Him who Loves God

> *"There is no peace to the wicked, saith the Lord."*   Isaias 48:22
> *"Much peace have they that love Thy law."*   Psalms 118:165

FIRST POINT

All men in this life labor to find peace. The merchant, the soldier, he who has a lawsuit labors, hoping by that gain, that dignity, that lawsuit won, to make a fortune. and thus to find peace—but poor worldlings, who seek peace in the world which cannot give it! God alone can give us peace: "Give to Thy servants (prays the holy Church) that peace which the world cannot give." No, the world, with all its riches, cannot satisfy the heart of man, because man is not created for these things, but for God alone, so that God alone can satisfy him. Animals are created for the pleasures of sense, and they find peace in the good things of this earth. Give a horse a bundle of grass, or a dog a morsel of meat, and behold they are content; they desire nothing more. But the soul, which is created only to love and to be united to God, can never find peace though in the enjoyment of every sensual pleasure; God alone can fully satisfy her.

The rich man, mentioned in *Luke* (12:19), having gathered an abundant crop from his fields, said to himself: "Soul, thou hast much goods laid up for many years; take thy rest, eat, drink, make good cheer." But the unhappy man was called a fool; and with reason, says St. Basil: "Miserable wretch (says the saint to him), hast thou perchance the soul of some hog, some brute, that thou thinnest to satisfy thy soul by eating, drinking, and sensual pleasures?" A man, says St. Bernard, may be filled with the good things of this world, but not be satisfied: "He may be puffed up, but cannot be satisfied." And the same saint, writing upon this passage of the Gospel, "Behold we have left all things," observes, that he had seen divers madmen afflicted in various ways. All these, he says, suffered from a great hunger: but some satiated themselves with earth, which is a figure of the avaricious; some with air, which is a figure of those who aspire to honors; some, around a furnace, swallowed the sparks that flew from it, which is a figure of the angry; others, in fine, around a fetid lake, drank of its putrid waters, which is a figure of the unchaste. Then, turning to them, the saint exclaims: O fools, do you not perceive that these things rather increase than satisfy your hunger? The goods of the world are but apparent goods, and cannot therefore satisfy the heart of man: "You have eaten, but have not had enough." (*Agg.* 1:6). The more, therefore, an avaricious man acquires, the more he endeavors to acquire. St. Augustine says: "The accumulation of money does not close, but widens, the jaws of avarice." The more the unchaste wallows in filth, the more is he at the same time nauseated and yet hungered; and how, indeed, can dung and sensual filth content the heart? The same happens to the ambitious, who try to satisfy their desires with mere smoke, since they look more to what they want than to what they have. Alexander the Great, after having won so many kingdoms, wept because he had no more to conquer. If the goods of this world could content man, the rich, the monarchs of the earth, would be fully happy; but experience proves the contrary. Solomon declares it, who asserts that he had denied nothing to his senses: "Whatsoever my eyes desired, I refused them not." (*Ecclus.* 2:10). But for all that, what says he? "Vanity of vanities, and all is vanity." (*Ecclus.* 1:2). By which he means: All that is in the world is mere vanity, a mere lie, mere folly.

AFFECTIONS AND PRAYERS

Ah, my God, what remains now for me of all my offenses against Thee but pains, bitterness, and merits for Hell? I regret not the bitterness I now feel; on the contrary, it consoles me, since it is the gift of Thy grace, and gives me cause to hope (since it is Thyself who bestowest it on me) that Thou wilt pardon me. What afflicts me is, the grief I have occasioned Thee, my Redeemer, who hast so much loved me. I deserved, O my Lord, that Thou shouldst then abandon me; but instead of this, Thou dost offer me pardon, nay, Thou art the first to seek for a reconciliation. Yes, my Jesus, I long for peace, and desire Thy grace above every other blessing. I grieve for having offended Thee, O Infinite Goodness, and I would willingly die of sorrow. Oh, by that love which Thou didst bear me when dying for me on the cross, pardon me, and receive me into Thy Heart; and change my heart so that I may in future please Thee as much as I have hitherto displeased Thee. For Thy love I now renounce all the pleasures that the world can give me, and I resolve rather to lose my life than Thy grace. Tell me what I must do to please Thee, and I will do it. What care I for pleasures, honors, riches! I desire Thee only, my God, my joy, my glory, my treasure, my life, my love, my all.

Give me, Lord, Thy help, that I may be faithful to Thee. Grant that I may love Thee, and do with me what Thou wilt. Mary, my Mother, and my hope after Jesus, take me under thy protection, and make me belong wholly to God.

SECOND POINT

Not only does Solomon say, that the pleasures and riches of this world are but vanities that cannot satisfy the heart, but that they are pains which afflict the spirit: "Behold, all is vanity and affliction of spirit." (*Eccles.* 1:14). Poor sinners! they think to gain happiness by their sins, but they find only bitterness and remorse: "Destruction and unhappiness in their ways, and the way of peace they have not known." (*Psalms* 13:3). Peace! What peace? No, says God: "There is no peace for the wicked." (*Isaias* 48:22). In the first place, sin brings with it the terror of Divine vengeance. If anyone has a powerful enemy, he can neither eat, nor sleep in peace; and can he who has God for an enemy rest in peace? "Fear to them that work evil." (*Prov.* 10:29). If there is an earthquake, or if it thunders, how does he tremble who is living in sin? Every leaf that moves alarms him: "The sound of dread is always in his ears." (*Job* 15:21). He is ever flying though he sees not who pursues him: "The wicked man fleeth when no man pursueth." (*Prov.* 28:1). And who pursues him? His own sin. Cain, after he had killed his brother Abel, said: "Every one, therefore, that findeth me shall kill me." (*Gen.* 4:14). And although the Lord assured him that no one would injure him—"No, it shall not be so"—yet, says the Scripture, Cain was always a fugitive from one place to another: "He dwelt as a fugitive on the earth." (*Gen.* 4:16). Who persecuted Cain but his own sin?

Moreover, sin brings with it remorse of conscience; that cruel worm that gnaws without ceasing. The wretched sinner goes to the play, the ball, the banquet; but, says his conscience, Thou art in enmity with God;

and if thou wert to die whither wouldst thou go? Remorse of conscience is so great a torment even in this life, that to rid themselves of it, some have even deliberately destroyed themselves. One of these, as we all know, was Judas, who hung himself in despair. It is related of another, that having killed a child, he became a religious, to fly from the pain of remorse of conscience; but not having found peace even in religion, he went and confessed his crime to the judge, and caused himself to be condemned to death.

What is a soul that lives without God? The Holy Spirit compares it to a stormy sea: "The wicked are like the raging sea, which cannot rest." (*Isaias* 57:20). I ask of you, if anyone were taken to a musical festival, or to a ball or feast, and there to be hung by the feet, with his head downwards, could he enjoy this amusement? Such is the man who lives with his soul turned upside down, being in the midst of the enjoyments of this world, but without God. He may eat, and drink, and dance; he may wear to great advantage that rich dress, receive those honors, obtain that dignity, or those possessions; but peace he will never have: "There is no peace for the wicked." Peace comes from God alone; and God gives it to His friends, not to His enemies.

The pleasures of this earth, says St. Vincent Ferrer, run out; they enter not into the heart: "They are waters which do not penetrate where there is thirst." The sinner may wear a rich embroidered robe, or a splendid diamond on his finger; he may indulge the sense of taste according to his inclination; but his poor heart will remain full of thorns and bitterness; therefore shalt thou behold her, with all his riches, pleasures, and amusements, always unquiet, and at every contradiction infuriated and angry, like a mad dog. He who loves God resigns himself under adverse events to the Divine Will, and finds peace; but he cannot do this who is an enemy to the will of God, and therefore he has no way of tranquillising himself. The unhappy man serves the devil—serves a tyrant, who repays him with grief and bitterness. Ah, the word of God cannot fail, which says: "Because thou didst not serve the Lord thy God with joy and gladness, thou shalt serve thy enemy in hunger and thirst and nakedness, and in want of all things." (*Deut.* 28:48). What does not that revengeful man suffer when he has avenged himself! That unchaste man when he has gained his object! That ambitious, that avaricious man! Oh, how many, did they but suffer for God what they suffer in order to damn themselves, would become great saints!

AFFECTIONS AND PRAYERS

O my lost life! O my God, had I but suffered to serve Thee the pains that I have suffered to offend Thee, how many merits should I now have in store for Heaven! Ah, my Lord, for what did I leave Thee, and lose Thy grace? For brief and empoisoned pleasures, which vanished almost as soon as possessed, and which left my heart full of thorns and bitterness. Ah, my sins, I detest and curse you a thousand times; and I bless Thy mercy, O my God, which has borne so patiently with me. I love Thee, O my Creator and Redeemer, who hast given Thy life for me; and because I love Thee, I repent with all my heart of having offended Thee. My God, my God, why have I lost Thee; and for what have I exchanged Thee? I now know the evil I have done; and I resolve to lose everything, even life itself, rather than Thy love. Give me light, Eternal Father, for the love of Jesus Christ; make me know how great a good Thou art, and how vile are those pleasures which the devil offers me to make me lose Thy grace. I love Thee; but I desire to love Thee more. Grant that Thou mayest be my only thought, my only desire, my only love. I hope all things from Thy goodness, through the merits of Thy Son, Mary, my Mother, through the love thou bearest to Jesus Christ, I implore thee to obtain for me light and strength to serve Him, and to love Him until death.

Third Point

Since, then, all the goods and pleasures of the world cannot satisfy the heart of man, what can satisfy it? God alone: "Delight in the Lord, and he will give thee the requests of thy heart." (*Psalms* 36:4). The heart of man is ever in search of that good which may satisfy it. It obtains riches, pleasures, honors, and is not content, because these are finite goods, and it is created for an infinite good: let it find God, let it unite itself to God, and behold it is content, it desires nothing more: "Delight in the Lord, and he will give thee the requests of thy heart." St. Augustine found no peace during all the years he spent amidst the pleasures of sense. When he afterwards gave himself to God, he then confessed, and said to the Lord: "Our heart is unquiet until it finds its rest in Thee." My God, I now know that all is vanity and affliction, and that Thou alone art the true peace of the soul: "All things are full of trouble; Thou alone art repose." And thus having learned at his own cost, he writes: "What dost thou seek, O wretched man, in seeking for good things? Seek the one good, in which are all goods." David, when he was king, had recourse whilst he was in sin to the chase, to his gardens, to the table, and to all other royal pleasures; but the table, the gardens, and all the other creatures which he enjoyed, said to him: "David, dost thou think to be made happy by us?" No, we cannot satisfy thee. "Where is thy God?" Go, and find thy God, for He alone can satisfy thee. Therefore, in the midst of all his enjoyments, David did nothing but weep: "My tears have been my bread day and night, whilst it is said to me daily: Where is thy God?" (*Psalms* 41:4).

But oh, how happy, on the other hand, does God make those faithful souls that love Him! St. Francis of Assisi, having left all for God, although his feet were naked, his covering was a rag, and he half-dead with cold and hunger, experienced the joys of paradise, saying: "My God and my all." St. Francis Borgia, after he became a religious, and was obliged in his travels to lie upon straw, received such great consolations, that he could not sleep. So also St. Philip Neri, having left all things, God gave him such consolation when he went to rest, that he even exclaimed: "But, my Jesus, let me sleep." Father Charles of Lorraine, a Jesuit, of the princes of Lorraine, when he found himself in his poor cell, would sometimes begin to dance through joy. St. Francis Xavier, in the plains of India, uncovered his breast, saying: "It is enough, O Lord; no more consolation, for my heart is not capable of enduring it." St. Teresa said, that one drop of heavenly consolation gives more happiness than all the pleasures and amusements of the world. Ah, God cannot fail in His promises to give to him who leaves the goods of this world for the love of Him a hundredfold, even in this life, of peace and contentment: "Every one that hath left house, or brethren, or sisters, or father, or mother, or children, or lands, for my name's sake, shall receive a hundredfold, and shall possess life everlasting." (*Matt.* 19:29).

What, then, do we seek? Let us go to Jesus Christ, who calls us and says: "Come to me all you that labor and are burdened, and I will refresh you." (*Matt.* 11:28). Ah, the soul that loves God finds that peace which surpasses all the pleasures and gratifications which the senses and the world can give: "The peace of God, which surpasseth all understanding." (*Phil.* 4:7). It is true that in this life even the saints suffer, because this earth is the place of merits, and we cannot merit without suffering; but, says St. Bonaventure, Divine love is like honey, which makes the most bitter things sweet and amiable. He who loves God loves His will, and therefore rejoices in spirit even in the midst of afflictions, because in embracing them he knows that he pleases Him and gives Him pleasure. O God, sinners despise a spiritual life; but they do not try it: They see the cross, but they do not see its unction. They

look only, says St. Bernard, to the mortifications
endured by the lovers of God, and the pleasures of
which they deprive themselves; but they perceive not
the spiritual delights with which the Lord caresses
them. Oh, that sinners would taste the peace which a
soul enjoys who desires nothing but God! "Taste and
see (says David) that the Lord is sweet." (*Psalms* 33:9).
My brother, begin now to make daily meditation, to
communicate often, to visit the most holy Sacrament;
begin to leave the world, and to reconcile yourself with
God; and you will find that the Lord will give you more
consolation in that short time which you spend with
Him than the world has given you with all its amusements: "Taste and see." He who does not taste, cannot
understand what happiness God bestows on a soul that
loves Him.

AFFECTIONS AND PRAYERS

My dear Redeemer, how have I hitherto been so blind
as to leave Thee, the infinite Good, the Fountain of all
consolations, for the miserable and brief gratifications
of sense! I am amazed at my blindness; but I am still
more amazed at Thy mercy, which has borne with me
with so much goodness, I thank Thee for making me
now perceive my folly, and my obligation to love Thee,
I love Thee, O my Jesus, with all my soul; and I desire
to love Thee more. Do Thou increase this desire and
this love. Enamor my soul of Thee, who art infinitely
amiable, who hast left nothing undone to inspire me
with love for Thee, and who so desirest my love. "If
Thou wilt, Thou canst make me clean." Ah, my dear
Redeemer, purify my heart from those many impure
affections that hinder me from loving Thee as I could
wish. It is not in my power to make my heart burn
with Thy love, and love nothing but Thee; it must be
through the power of Thy grace, which can do all that
it wills. Detach me from all things, banish from my
soul every affection that is not for Thee, and make me

wholly Thine, I grieve, above all other evils, for the displeasure I have given Thee, and I resolve to consecrate the remainder of my life entirely to Thy holy love. But Thou must enable me to do this. Do it by that Blood which Thou hast shed for me with so much pain and so much love. Let it be the glory of Thy power, that my heart, which was once filled with earthly affections, be now all inflamed with the love of Thee, my Infinite Good. O Mother of fair love, make me, by thy prayers, be, as thou ever wert, all on fire with the love of God.

CONSIDERATION XII

On the Habit of Sin

"The wicked man, when he is come into the depth of sins, contemneth."
Proverbs 18:3

FIRST POINT

One of the greatest ills which the sin of Adam brought upon us was the evil inclination to sin. This made the Apostle weep when he found himself impelled by concupiscence towards those very sins which he abhorred: "I see another law in my members . . . captivating me in the law of sin." (*Rom.* 7:23). Therefore is it so difficult for us, infected as we are by this concupiscence, and with so many enemies urging us to evil, to arrive without sin at our heavenly country. Now such being our frailty, I ask, what should you say of a voyager who, having to cross the sea in a great storm, in a shattered bark, would load it in such a manner as would be sufficient to sink it even were there no storm and the vessel strong? What would you predict as to the life of that man? Now we may say the same of the habitual sinner, who, having to pass the sea of this

life—a stormy sea, in which so many are lost—in a
frail and shattered bark, such as is our flesh to which
we are united, still burdens it with habitual sins. Such
a one can hardly be saved, because a bad habit blinds
the understanding, hardens the heart, and thus renders him obstinate to the last.

In the first place, a bad habit produces *blindness.*
And why, indeed, do the saints always beg for light
from God, trembling lest they should become the worst
sinners in the world? Because they know that if for
a moment they lose that light, there is no enormity
they may not commit. How is it that so many Christians have lived obstinately in sin until at last they
have damned themselves? "Their own malice blinded
them." (*Wis.* 2:21). Sin deprived them of sight, and
thus they were lost. Every sin produces blindness; and
as sin increases, so does the blindness increase. God
is our light; as much, therefore, as the soul withdraws
from God, so much the more blind does she become:
"His bones shall be filled with the vices of his youth."
(*Job* 20:11). As in a vessel full of earth the light of
the sun cannot penetrate, so in a heart full of vices
Divine light cannot enter. Therefore do we see certain
relapsed sinners lose all light, and proceed from sin
to sin, without any more even thinking of amendment:
"The wicked walk round about." (*Psalms* 11:9). Having fallen into that dark pit, the unhappy wretches
can do nothing but sin; they speak only of sin; they
think only of sin; and hardly perceive at last what
harm there is in sin. The very habit of committing sin
(says St. Augustine) prevents sinners from perceiving
the evil they do. So that they live as if they no longer
believed in God, in Heaven, in Hell, or in eternity.

And behold, that sin which at first struck with terror, through ill habit no longer causes horror: "Make
them like a wheel, and as stubble before the wind."
(*Psalms* 82:14). Behold, says St. Gregory, with what
ease a straw is stirred by the slightest wind; thus also
you will see one who before he fell resisted, at least

for some time, and combated temptation, when the bad habit is contracted fall instantly at every temptation, and on every occasion that presents itself of sin. And why? Because the bad habit has deprived him of light. St. Anselm says, that the devil acts with some sinners like one who holds a bird tied by a string; he allows it to fly, but, when he chooses, he drags it to the earth again. So is it, says the saint, with habitual sinners: "Entangled by a bad habit, they are bound by the enemy; and though flying, they are cast down into the same vices."[43] Some, adds St. Bernardine of Sienna, continue to sin, even without occasion.[44] The saint compares habitual sinners to windmills, which turn with every breath of air; and moreover go round, even though there be not a grain of corn to grind, and the master should wish them to stop. You will see an habitual sinner without occasion indulging in bad thoughts, without pleasure, and almost without will, drawn forcibly on by bad habit. As St. John Chrysostom observes, "Habit is a merciless thing; it forces men, sometimes even against their will, to the commission of unlawful acts." Yes, because (according to St. Augustine) bad habit becomes at last a sort of necessity: "When no resistance is made to a habit, it becomes a necessity." And, as St. Bernardine adds: "Habit is changed into nature." Hence, as it is necessary for a man to breathe, so to habitual sinners, who have made themselves slaves to sin, it appears almost necessary that they should sin. I have used the expression of *slaves;* there are servants who serve for pay, but slaves serve by force and without pay: to this do some poor wretches come, who at last sin without pleasure.

"The wicked man, when he is come to the depth of sins, contemneth." (*Prov.* 18:3). St. Chrysostom explains this of the habitual sinner, who, plunged into that pit of darkness, despises corrections, sermons, censures, Hell, God—despises all, and becomes like the vulture, which, rather than leave the dead body, allows itself to be killed upon it. Father Recupito relates, that a criminal on his way to execution raised his eyes, beheld a young girl, and consented to a bad thought. Father Gisolfo also relates, that a blasphemer, likewise condemned to death, uttered a blasphemy as he was thrown off the ladder. St. Bernard goes so far as to say, that it is of no use praying for habitual sinners, but we must weep for them as lost. How can they, indeed, avoid the precipice if they no longer see? It requires a miracle of grace. These unhappy beings will open their eyes in Hell, when it will be of no avail to open them, unless it be to weep the more bitterly over their folly.

AFFECTIONS AND PRAYERS

My God, Thou hast conferred signal blessings upon me, favoring me above others; and I have signally offended Thee by outraging Thee more than any other person known to me. O sorrowful Heart of my Redeemer, afflicted and tormented on the cross by the sight of my sins, give me, through Thy merits, a lively sense of my offenses, and sorrow for them. Ah, my Jesus, I am full of vices; but Thou art omnipotent, Thou canst easily fill my soul with Thy holy love. In Thee, then, I trust; Thou who art infinite goodness and infinite mercy. I repent, O my Sovereign Good, of having offended Thee. Oh, that I had rather died, and had never caused Thee any displeasure! I have forgotten Thee; but Thou hast not forgotten me; I perceive it by the light Thou now givest me. Since, then, Thou givest me light, give me likewise strength to be faithful to Thee. I promise Thee rather to die a thousand times than ever again to turn my back on Thee. But all my hopes are in Thy assistance: "In Thee, O Lord, have I hoped; let me not be confounded forever." I hope in Thee, my Jesus, never again to find myself entangled in iniquity and deprived of Thy grace. To thee also do I turn, O Mary, my blessed Lady: "In thee, O Lady, have I hoped; let me not be confounded forever." O my hope, I trust by thy intercession that I may never again find myself in enmity with thy Son. Ah, beg of Him rather to let me die than that He should abandon me to this greatest of misfortunes.

SECOND POINT

A bad habit moreover *hardens the heart:* "The habit of sin hardens the heart;"[45] and God justly permits it in punishment of resistance to His calls. The Apostle says, that the Lord "hath mercy on whom he will; and whom he will he hardeneth." (*Rom.* 9:18). St. Augustine explains it thus: It is not that God hardens the habitual sinner; but He withdraws His grace in punishment of his ingratitude for past graces, and thus his heart becomes hard and as a stone: "His heart shall be as hard as a stone, and as firm as a smith's anvil." (*Job* 41:15). Hence, when others are moved and weep on hearing sermons on the rigors of Divine justice, the pains of the damned, and the passion of Jesus Christ, the habitual sinner is in no way affected; he will speak of these things, and hear them spoken of, with indifference, as if they were things that concerned him not; and he will only become more hardened: "He shall be as firm as a smith's anvil." Even sudden deaths, earthquakes, thunderbolts, and lightning, will no longer terrify him; instead of arousing him, and making him enter into himself, they will rather produce in him that stupor of death in which he hopelessly sleeps: "At thy rebuke, O God of Jacob, they have all slumbered." (*Psalms* 75:7). A bad habit by degrees destroys even remorse of conscience. To the habitual sinner the most enormous sins appear as nothing, says St. Augustine: "Sins, however horrible, when once habitual, seem little or no sin at all." The commission of sin naturally carries along with it a certain shame; but, says St. Jerome, "Habitual sinners lose even shame in sinning." St. Peter compares the habitual sinner to the swine that wallows in the mire. (*2 Peter* 2:22). As the swine that rolls in the mire perceives not the stench, so is it with the habitual sinner; that stench, which is perceived by all others, is unnoticed by him alone. And, supposing the mire to have deprived him also of sight, what wonder is it, says St. Bernardine, that he amends not even when God chastises him! "The people wallow in sin, as the sow in a pool of filth; what wonder is it if they perceive not the coming judgments of an avenging God!"[46] Hence, instead of grieving over his sins, he rejoices in them, he laughs at them, he boasts of them: "They are glad when they have done evil." "A fool worketh mischief, as it were, for sport." (*Prov.* 2:14; 10:23). What signs are not these of diabolical obduracy! They are all signs of damnation, says St. Thomas of Villanova: "Hardness of heart is the sign of damnation." My brother, tremble lest the same should happen to you. If perchance you have any bad habit, endeavor to break from it speedily, now that God calls you. And as long as your conscience smites you, rejoice; for it is a sign that God has not yet abandoned you. But amend, and leave it quickly; for if not, the wound will become gangrenous, and you will be lost.

AFFECTIONS AND PRAYERS

How can I thank Thee, O Lord, as I ought for the many graces Thou hast bestowed on me! How often hast Thou called me, and I have resisted! Instead of being grateful to Thee, and loving Thee for having delivered me from Hell, and called me with so much love, I have continued to provoke Thy wrath by requiting Thee with insults No, my God, I will no longer outrage Thy patience; I have offended Thee enough. Thou alone, who art infinite love, couldst have borne with me till now. But I now see that Thou canst bear with me no longer; and with reason. Pardon, then, my Lord and my Sovereign Good, all my offenses against Thee; of which I repent with my whole heart, for I purpose in future never to offend Thee again. What! Shall I perchance always continue to provoke Thee? Ah, be appeased with me, O God of my soul; not through my merits, for which vengeance and Hell alone are reserved, but through the merits of Thy Son and my Redeemer, in which I place my hope. For the love, then, of Jesus Christ receive me into Thy grace, and give me perseverance in Thy love. Detach me from all impure affections, and draw me wholly to Thee. I love Thee, O great God, O Supreme Lover of souls, worthy of infinite love. Oh, that I had always loved Thee! O Mary, my Mother, grant that the remainder of my life may be spent, not in offending thy Son, but only in loving Him, and weeping over the displeasure I have caused Him.

THIRD POINT

When light is lost, and the heart is hardened, the probable consequence will be that the sinner will make a bad end, and die *obstinate in his sin:* "A hard heart shall fare evil at the last." (*Ecclus.* 3:27). The just continue to walk in the straight road: "The path of the just is right to walk in." (*Isaias* 26:7). Habitual sinners, on the contrary, go always in a circle: "The wicked walk round about." (*Psalms* 11:9). They leave sin for a while, and then they return to it. To such as these St. Bernard announces damnation: "Woe to the man who follows this circle!" Such a one will say: I will amend before I die. But the difficulty lies in this, that an habitual sinner should amend even though he attain to old age. The Holy Spirit says: "A young man according to his way, even when he is old he will not depart from it." (*Prov.* 22:6). The reason is, according to St. Thomas of Villanova, that our strength is very feeble: "Your strength shall be as the ashes of tow." (*Isaias* 1:31). From which it follows, as the saint observes, that the soul, deprived of grace, cannot avoid committing fresh sins: "Hence it comes to pass, that the soul, destitute of grace, cannot long escape fresh sins."[48] But besides this, what madness would it be in a person to play and lose voluntarily all he possessed, in the hope of winning it back at the last stake! Such is the folly of those who continue to live in sin, and hope at the last moment of their life to repair all. Can the Ethiopian or the leopard change the color of their skin? And how can he lead a good life who has contracted a long habit of sin? "If the Ethiopian can change his skin, or the leopard his spots, you also may do well when you have learned evil." (*Jer.* 13:23). Hence it happens that the habitual sinner abandons himself at last to despair, and thus ends his life. (*Prov.* 14:28).

St. Gregory, on that passage of Job, "He hath torn me with wound upon wound, he hath rushed in upon me like a giant." (*Job* 16:15), remarks: "If a person is attacked by an enemy, he is perhaps able to defend himself at the first wound he receives; but the more wounds that are inflicted on her, the more strength does he lose, until he is at last overcome and killed." Thus is it with sin: after the first, after the second time, the sinner has still some strength left (always, be it understood, through the means of grace, which assists him); but if he continues to sin, sin becomes a giant: "It rushes upon him as a giant." On the other hand, the sinner being weaker, and covered with wounds, how can he escape death? Sin, according to Jeremias is like a heavy stone that weighs upon the soul: "They have laid a stone over me." (*Lam.* 3:53). Now St. Bernard says, that it is as difficult for an habitual sinner to rise, as for one who has fallen under a heavy stone, and who has not strength sufficient to remove it, to free himself from it; "He rises with difficulty who is pressed down by the mass of a bad habit."

But the habitual sinner will exclaim, Then my case is desperate? No, not desperate, if you wish to amend. But well does a certain author observe, that great ills require great remedies: "It is good in severe diseases to commence the cure by severe remedies."[49] If a physician were to say to a sick man in danger of death, who refused to apply proper remedies, being ignorant of the serious nature of his malady, "My friend, you are a dead man unless you take such a medicine;" how would the sick man reply? "Behold me," he would say, "ready to take any thing; my life is at stake." Dear Christian, I say the same to you: if you have contracted the habit of some sin, you are in a bad way, and of the number of those sick men who "are rarely cured," according to St. Thomas of Villanova. You are on the brink of perdition. If, however, you wish to recover, there is a remedy: but you must not expect a miracle of grace; you must on your side do violence to yourself, you must fly from dangerous occasions, avoid bad company, and resist when you are tempted, recommending yourself to God. You must make use of proper means, going frequently to confession, reading every day a spiritual book, practicing devotion to the Blessed Virgin, praying constantly to her that she may obtain for you strength not to relapse. You must do violence to yourself, otherwise the threat of the Lord against the obstinate will be fulfilled in your regard: "You shall die in your sin." (*John* 8:21). And if you do not amend now that God gives you light, it will be more difficult to do so later. Hear God, who calls you: "Lazarus, come forth." Poor sinner, already dead, come out of the dark grave of your bad life. Reply quickly, give yourself to God, and tremble lest this should be your last call.

Affections and Prayers

Ah, my God, shall I, then, wait till Thou dost absolutely abandon me, and send me to Hell? Ah, Lord, wait for me; for I am resolved to change my life, and give myself to Thee. Tell me what I must do, and I will do it, O Blood of Jesus, aid me. O Mary, Advocate of sinners, succor me; and Thou, Eternal Father, through the merits of Jesus and Mary, have pity on me. I repent, O God of infinite goodness, of having offended Thee; and I love Thee above all things. Pardon me, for the

love of Jesus Christ, and give me Thy love. Give me
also a great fear of my eternal perdition should I again
offend Thee. Light, O my God—light and strength! I
hope for all through Thy mercy. Thou hast bestowed
on me so many graces when I wandered far from Thee;
how much more, then, may I hope now that I return
to Thee, resolved to love Thee alone. I love Thee, my
God, my life, my all. I love thee also, O Mary, my
Mother; to thee I consign my soul; preserve it by thy
intercession from again falling into disgrace with God.

CONSIDERATION XIII

The Delusions Which the Devil
Suggests to the Minds of Sinners

(Although many of the sentiments con-
tained in this Consideration are to be found
in the preceding ones, it is nevertheless
useful to collect them together, in order to
overcome the usual delusions which the
devil makes use of to induce sinners to
relapse).

FIRST POINT

Let us imagine a young person who has fallen into
grievous sins, has confessed them, and has regained
Divine grace. The devil again tempts him to fall: he
still resists, but already wavers through the deceits
suggested to him by the enemy. Young man, I say, tell
me, what will you do? Will you now lose the grace of
God, which you have regained, and which is of more
value than the whole world, for this wretched gratification? Will you write your own sentence of eternal
death, and condemn yourself to burn forever in Hell?
"No," you say, "I do not wish to condemn myself, I
wish to be saved; if I commit this sin, I will after-

wards confess it." Behold the first delusion of the
tempter. You say to me, then, that you will afterwards
confess it? But in the mean time you already lose
your soul. Tell me, if you had in your hand a jewel
worth a thousand ducts, would you throw it into the
river, saying, Afterwards I will search diligently, and
I hope to find it? You hold in your hand that precious
jewel of your soul, which Jesus Christ has purchased
by His Blood; and you cast it voluntarily into Hell
(for in sinning you are, according to present justice,
already condemned), and say, But I hope to recover
it by confession. But supposing you should not recover
it? To recover it you must have true repentance, which
is the gift of God; and if God should not give you this
repentance? and if death were to come, and take from
you time for confession?

You say you will not allow a week to pass over without confession; and who promises you this week? You
say you will go to confession tomorrow; and who promises you this tomorrow? St. Augustine says: "God has
not promised you tomorrow; perhaps He will give it
you, and perhaps He will deny it you," as He has denied
it to so many, who have gone to bed alive at night,
and have been found dead in the morning. How many
has God struck dead and sent to Hell in the very act
of sinning!

And should He do the same to you, how can you
ever repair your eternal ruin? Know, that through this
delusion, "I will confess afterwards," the devil has carried off thousands and thousands of Christians to Hell;
since we shall hardly find a sinner so desperate as
positively to resolve to damn himself: all, even when
they commit sin, do so in the hope of future confession. But thus have so many poor souls been lost, and
now they can no longer repair the past.

But you say, "At present I do not feel strength to
resist this temptation." Behold the second delusion of
the devil, who makes it appear to you impossible to
resist the present passion. In the first place, you must

know that God, as the Apostle says, is faithful, and never permits us to be tempted above our strength: "God is faithful, who will not suffer you to be tempted above that which you are able." (*1 Cor.* 10:13). I ask of you moreover, if you are not confident now of being able to resist, how can you hope to resist hereafter? Hereafter the devil will not fail to tempt you to other sins; and then he will have become much stronger against you, and you will be weaker. If, then, you feel you cannot now extinguish this flame, how can you hope to do so where it will be infinitely greater? You say, God will aid me. But God aids you now; why, then, with this aid will you not resist? Do you hope perchance that God will increase His aids and His graces after you have increased the number of your sins? And if you now require greater help and strength, why do you not ask it of God? Do you perchance doubt of the faithfulness of God, who has promised to give all that is asked of Him? "Ask, and it shall be given to you." (*Matt.* 7:7). God cannot fail; have recourse to Him, and He will give you that strength which you need to resist. "God does not command impossibilities," says the Council of Trent; "but by commanding both admonishes thee to do what thou art able, and to pray for what thou art not able (to do), and aids thee that thou mayest be able."[50] God does not command us what is impossible; but in imposing on us His precepts He admonishes us to do what we can with the actual aid He bestows on us; and should that aid prove insufficient for us to resist, He exhorts us to ask for more aid; and if we ask for it properly, He will certainly give it to us.

PRAYER

Is it, then, O my God, because Thou hast been so good to me, that I have been thus ungrateful to Thee? We have been engaged in a contest—I to fly from Thee, and Thou to pursue me; Thou to do me good, and I to return Thee evil. Ah, my Lord, were there no other reason, Thy goodness alone towards me ought to enamor me of Thee, since whilst I have increased my sins, Thou hast increased Thy graces. And how have I merited the light Thou now givest me? My Lord, I thank Thee for it with my whole heart; and I hope to thank Thee for it for all eternity in Heaven. I hope to be saved through Thy Blood; and I hope it with certainty, since Thou hast shown me such great mercy. In the meantime I hope Thou wilt give me strength never more to betray Thee. I purpose, with Thy grace, to (lie a thousand times rather than offend Thee any more. I have offended Thee enough; during the remainder of my life I will love Thee. And how can I but love a God, who, after having died for me, has borne with me so patiently, in spite of the many injuries I have done Him! O God of my soul, I repent with all my heart; I wish I could die of sorrow. But if in the past I have turned my back on Thee, I now love Thee above all things; I love Thee more than myself. Eternal Father, through the merits of Jesus Christ, succor a miserable sinner, who desires to love Thee. Mary, my hope, assist me; obtain for me the grace to have recourse always to thy Son and to thee whenever the devil tempts me to offend Her again.

SECOND POINT

The sinner says, "God is merciful." Behold the third ordinary delusion of sinners, by which great numbers are lost. A learned author declares that the mercy of God sends more souls to Hell than His justice; because these unhappy ones, confiding rashly in His mercy, continue in sin, and are thus lost. God is merciful. Who denies it? Nevertheless how many does He daily send to Hell? He is merciful; but He is also just, and He is therefore obliged to punish those who offend Him. He shows mercy; but to whom? To him that fears Him: "His mercy is towards them that fear Her." "The Lord hath compassion on them that fear him." (*Psalms* 102:11, 13).

But as for those who despise Him, and abuse His mercy only to despise Him the more, He exercises justice in their regard. And with reason. God pardons the sin; but He cannot pardon the determination to sin. St. Augustine says, that he who sins with the intention of repenting afterwards, is not a penitent, but a mocker of God. On the other hand, the Apostle tells us that God will not be mocked: "Be not deceived, God is not mocked." (*Galatians* 6:7). It would be mocking God to offend Him as we please and when we please, and then to expect Heaven.

"But as God has hitherto shown me so many mercies, and has not punished me, so I hope He will show me mercy in future." Behold the fourth delusion. Because, then, God has had compassion on you, therefore is He always to show compassion to you, and never to chastise you? On the contrary, the greater the mercies He has shown you have been, so much the more ought you to tremble lest He should pardon you no more, and chastise you if you offend Him again. "Say not," we are told in Ecclesiasticus—"Say not, I have sinned, and what harm hath befallen me? for the Most High is a patient rewarder." (*Ecclus.* 5:4); I have sinned, and have not been punished, for God endures; but He does not endure forever. When the limit fixed by Him for the mercies He intends to show a sinner is attained, He then punishes all his sins together. And the longer He has waited for his repentance, so much the more severe will be his punishment; as says St. Gregory: "Those whom He waits for the longest, He punishes the most severely."

If, then, you perceive, my brother, that you have often offended God, and God has not cast you into Hell, you must say: "The mercies of the Lord that we are not consumed." (*Lam.* 3:22). Lord, I thank Thee that Thou hast not sent me to Hell, as I deserved. Consider how many have been condemned for less sins than you have committed, and remembering this, endeavor to atone for your offenses against God by penance and other good works. The patience that God has had with you ought to animate you not to displease Him still more, but to love and serve Him better than you have done; considering that He has shown you so many mercies, which He has not shown to others.

PRAYER

My crucified Jesus, my Redeemer and my God, behold a traitor at Thy feet. I am ashamed to appear before Thee. How often have I mocked Thee, how often have I promised never more to offend Thee! But my promises have all been treacherous; since, when the occasion presented itself, I forgot Thee, and again turned my back on Thee. I thank Thee that my abode at this moment is not in Hell; but that Thou permittest me to be at Thy feet instead, and enlightenest me, and callest me to Thy love. Yes, I am resolved to love Thee, my Saviour and my God, and never more to despise Thee. Thou hast borne with me long enough. I perceive that Thou canst bear with me no longer. Unhappy me, if after so many graces I should offend Thee again! Lord, I resolutely determine to change my life, and to love Thee as much as I have offended Thee. I rejoice that I have to deal with infinite goodness such as Thine. I repent above all things of having despised Thee as I have done, and I promise Thee all my love in future. Pardon me through the merits of Thy passion; forget the injuries I have done Thee; and give me strength to be faithful to Thee during the remainder of my life. I love Thee, O my Sovereign Good; and I hope to love Thee always. My dear Lord, I will leave Thee no more. O Mary, Mother of God, bind me to Jesus Christ; and obtain for me the grace never again to depart from His feet. In thee I confide.

THIRD POINT

"But I am young; God compassionates youth; hereafter I will give myself to God." We have now come to the fifth delusion. You are young. But do you not know that God counts not years, but the sins of each one? You are young. But how many sins have you fallen into? There may be many old people who have not been guilty even of the tenth part of the sins you have committed. And do you not know that God has fixed the number and the measure of the sins which He will pardon in each one? "The Lord waiteth patiently (says the Scripture), that when the day of judgment shall come, He may punish them (the nations) in the fullness of their sins." (*2 Mach.* 6:14). That is to say, God has patience, and waits up to a certain point; but when the measure of the sins which He has determined to pardon is full, He no longer pardons, but chastises the sinner, either by a sudden death in the state of damnation in which he then is, or by abandoning him to his sin—a punishment worse than death: "I will take away the hedge thereof, and it shall be wasted." (*Isaias* 5:5). If you have a piece of land which you have encompassed with a hedge of thorns, cultivated for many years, and expended much money upon, and you see that after all it yields no fruit, what do you do? You take away the hedge, and leave it to desolation. Tremble lest God should do the same to you. If you continue to sin, gradually you will cease to feel remorse of conscience; you will think no more of eternity nor of your soul; you will lose almost all light; you will lose all fear. Behold the hedge is taken away, behold God has already abandoned you.

Let us now come to the last delusion. You say: "It is true that by this sin I lose the grace of God, and I have condemned myself to Hell; it may be that for this sin shall be damned; but it may also be that I shall afterwards confess it, and be saved." True, I admit that you may yet he saved; for, after all, I am not a prophet, and cannot say for certain that after this sin God will no longer show mercy to you. But you cannot deny that, after so many graces which the Lord has bestowed on you, you will very likely be lost if you now return to offend Him. It is said in the Scriptures, "A hard heart shall fare evil at the last." (*Ecclus.* 3:27); "Evil-doers shall be cut off." (*Psalms* 36:9): evil-doers shall at last be cut off by Divine justice. "What things a man sows, those also shall he reap." (*Galatians* 6:8): he that sows in sins, in the end shall reap only pains and torments. "I have called, and you refused . . . I will laugh in your destruction and mock you." (*Prov.* 1:24, 26): I have called thee, says God, and thou hast mocked Me; but I will mock thee at the hour of death. "Revenge is mine, and I will repay in due time." (*Deut.* 32:35): vengeance is Mine, and I will repay when the time is come. Thus, then, do the Scriptures speak of obstinate sinners; such is what reason and justice require. You say to me: "But perhaps, after all, I shall be saved." And I repeat, Yes, perhaps; but what folly, I also say, to rest eternal salvation upon a *perhaps,* and upon a *perhaps* so uncertain! Is this an affair to be placed in such peril?

PRAYER

My dear Redeemer, prostrate at Thy feet I thank Thee for not having abandoned me after so many sins. What numbers, who have offended Thee less than I have, will never receive the light Thou now givest me! I perceive that truly Thou desirest my salvation; and I desire to be saved chiefly to please Thee. I desire to sing the many mercies Thou hast shown me for all eternity in Heaven. I hope that now, at this hour, Thou hast already pardoned me; but even should I be in disgrace with Thee, because I have not known how to repent of my offenses against Thee as I ought, I now repent of them with all my soul, and grieve for them above all other evils. Pardon me in Thy mercy, and increase in me more and more sorrow for having offended Thee, my God, who art so good. Give me sorrow, and give me love. I love Thee above all things, but I still love Thee too little; I wish to love Thee much; and I ask this love of Thee, and hope for it from Thee. Hear me, my Jesus; for Thou hast promised to hear those who call upon Thee. O Mary, Mother of God, all assure me that thou never sendest away disconsolate those who recommend themselves to thee. O my hope after Jesus, I fly to thee, and in thee I trust; recommend me to thy Son, and save me.

CONSIDERATION XIV

On the Particular Judgment

> *"We must all be manifested before the judgment-seat of Christ."*
> 2 Corinthians 5:10

FIRST POINT

Let us consider the soul's appearance before God—the accusation, the examination, and the sentence. And first, with regard to the appearance of the soul before the Judge: it is a common opinion amongst theologians that the particular judgment takes place at the very moment in which a man expires; and that in the very place where the soul is separated from the body, she is judged by Jesus Christ, who will not send, but will come Himself to judge her cause: "At what hour you think not the son of man will come." (*Luke* 12:40). "For the just He will come in love," says St. Augustine; "for the wicked in terror." Oh, what terror will he feel who beholds his Redeemer for the first time, and beholds Him in His wrath! "Who shall stand before the face of His indignation?" (*Nahum* 1:6). Reflecting upon this, Father Louis da Ponte trembled so as to shake his cell. The venerable Father Juvenal Ancina, on hearing the *Dies iræ* sung, at the thought of the terror which the soul will feel on being presented before the judgment-seat, resolved to leave the world; which resolution he carried into effect. The sight of the wrath of the Judge will be the forerunner of condemnation: "The wrath of a king is as messengers of death." (*Prov.* 16:14). St. Bernard says, that the soul will suffer more then in seeing the indignation of Jesus than in being in Hell itself: "She would rather be in Hell," Criminals have been known sometimes to fall into a cold sweat when brought into the presence of an earthly judge. Piso felt such confusion at appearing before the senate clothed as a criminal, that he committed suicide. What a grief is it to a child or to a subject to behold a parent or a prince seriously offended! But oh, how much greater a pain will it be to that soul to behold Jesus Christ, whom she despised during life! "They shall look on him whom they pierced." (*John* 19:37). That Lamb who in life had so much patience, the soul will then behold Him enraged, without any hope of appeasing Him; she will then call upon the mountains to fall upon her, and thus hide her from the fury of the wrathful Lamb: "Fall upon us, and hide us from the wrath of the lamb." (*Apoc.* 6:16). St. Luke, speaking of the judgment, says: "Then they shall see the Son of Man." (*Luke* 21:27). Oh, what torment will it be to the sinner to behold the Judge in the form of man! Because the sight of Him who as man died for his salvation will upbraid him the more forcibly with his ingratitude. When the Saviour ascended into Heaven, the angels said to the disciples: "This Jesus, who is taken up from you into heaven, shall so come as you have seen him going into heaven." (*Acts* 1:2). The Judge will then come with the same wounds with which He left the earth: "Great joy to the beholders, great terror to those who are in expectation," says the Abbot Rupert. Those wounds shall console the just, and terrify the wicked. When Joseph said to his brothers, "I am Joseph, whom you sold," the Scriptures say that through fear they were silent, and unable to speak: "His brethren could not answer him, being struck with exceeding great fear." (*Gen.* 45:3). How, then, will the sinner answer Jesus Christ? Will he dare ask for mercy, when he must first render an account of his abuse of past mercies? "With what face," says Eusebius Emissenus, "wilt thou ask for mercy, when thou must first be judged for the contempt of mercy?" "What, then, will he do," says St. Augustine? Whither will he fly when he beholds his angry Judge above, Hell open below, on one side his sins accusing him, on the other devils prepared to execute the sentence, and within him a remorseful conscience? "Above him will stand the indignant Judge, below the direful Hell, on his right his sins to accuse him, on his left devils to drag him to the place of torture, within him a burning conscience: whither, when thus straightened, shall the sinner fly?"

AFFECTIONS AND PRAYERS

O my Jesus, I will always call Thee Jesus; Thy name consoles me, encourages me, reminding me that Thou art my Saviour, who diedst for my salvation. Behold me at Thy feet. I acknowledge that I have deserved Hell as often as I have offended Thee by mortal sin. I am unworthy of pardon; but Thou hast died to obtain my pardon. *Recordare, Jesu pie, quod sum causa tuæ viæ.* Make haste, then, my Jesus, to pardon me before Thou comest to judge me. I can then no longer ask for mercy; but I can now ask for it, and hope to obtain it. Thy wounds will then fill me with terror; but now they give me confidence. My dear Redeemer, I grieve above all other evils for having offended Thy infinite goodness. I resolve to accept every pain and every loss rather than to lose Thy grace. I love Thee with all my heart. Have pity on me: "Have mercy upon me according to Thy great mercy." O Mary, Mother of Mercy, Advocate of sinners, obtain for me a great sorrow for my sins, and pardon and perseverance in Divine love. I love thee, O my Queen, and I trust in thee.

SECOND POINT

Consider the accusation, and the examination: "The judgment sat, and the books were opened." (*Dan.* 7:10). There shall be two books; the Gospel, and the conscience. In the Gospel will be read what the culprit ought to have done, and in the conscience what he has done. In the balance of Divine justice neither riches, nor dignities, nor nobility, but only works, will be weighed: "Thou art weighed in the balance," said Daniel to the King Balthassar, "and art found wanting." (*Dan.* 5:27). "Neither his gold, nor his riches, but the king only, was weighed," says Father Alvarez. Then will come the accusers; and first of all the devil. St. Augustine says: "The devil will stand before the tribunal of Christ, and will recite the words of thy profession. He will charge us to our face with all that we have done, the day and the hour in which we have sinned."[51] "He will recite the words of thy profession;" that is to say, he will bring forward our own promises, in which we have afterwards failed, and he will charge us with all our sins, pointing to the day and the hour in which we have committed them. Then will he say to the Judge, according to St. Cyprian: "I did not endure blows and scourging for these." Lord, I have suffered nothing for this culprit; but he left Thee, who hast died to save him, and made himself my slave; therefore he belongs to me. The guardian angels also will be accusers, according to Origen: "Each angel will bear witness to the number of years he has labored for him; but he despised every warning."[52] So that then "all his friends will despise him." (*Lam.* 1:2). The walls within which the offender has sinned will accuse him. "The stone shall cry out of the wall." (*Hab.* 2:11). His own conscience will accuse him: "Their conscience bearing witness to them in the day when God shall judge." (*Rom.* 2:15). His very sins, says St. Bernard, will speak, and say: "Thou hast made us, we are thy works; we will not abandon thee." Finally, according to St. Chrysostom, the wounds of Jesus

Christ will be accusers: "The nails will complain of thee; the wounds will speak against thee; the Cross of Christ will preach against thee." Then the examination will commence.

The Lord says: "At that time I will search Jerusalem with lamps." (*Soph.* 1:12). "The lamp," says Mendozza, "penetrates every corner" of the house. And Cornelius à Lapide, explaining these words, "with lamps," says, that God will then place before the culprit the examples of the saints, and all the lights and the inspirations which He has given him during life, as also all the years granted him for doing good: "He hath called against me the time." (*Lam.* 1:15). So that he will then have to render an account of every glance of the eye: "An account shall be exacted of thee, even to a glance of the eye," says St. Anselm. "He shall purify the sons of Levi." (*Mal.* 3:3). As gold is purified by separating it from the dross, in like manner will our good works be sifted, our confessions, our communions, etc. "When I shall take a time, I will judge justices." (*Psalms* 74:3). In short, St. Peter tells us, that in the judgment the just shall scarcely be saved: "And if the just man shall scarcely be saved, where shall the wicked and sinner appear?" (*Peter* 4:18). If we shall have to answer for every idle word, what account shall we have to render for so many bad thoughts consented to! So many improper words! "If for an idle word an account be demanded, what shall it be for a word of impurity!" says St. Gregory. The Lord specifically says (speaking of scandalous sinners, who have robbed Him of souls): "I will meet them as a bear that is robbed of her whelps." (*Osee* 13:8). Speaking of works, the Judge will say: "Give her of the fruit of her hands." (*Prov.* 31:31). Reward him according to the works which he has done.

AFFECTIONS AND PRAYERS

Ah, my Jesus, wert Thou now to reward me according to the works I have done, Hell would be my lot! O

God, how often have I myself written the sentence of my condemnation to that place of torments! I return Thee thanks for the patience with which Thou hast so long borne with me. O God, were I at this moment to appear before Thy tribunal, what account could I render Thee of my life? Ah, Lord, wait for me yet a little longer; do not judge me yet. If Thou wert now to judge me, what would become of me? Wait for me; since Thou hast shown me so many mercies hitherto, grant me this one more—give me a great sorrow for my sins. I repent, O my Sovereign Good, of having so often despised Thee. I love Thee above all things. Eternal Father, pardon me for the love of Jesus Christ; and through His merits grant me holy perseverance. My Jesus, I hope for all things through Thy blood, Most holy Mary, I trust in thee. "Turn, therefore, most gracious Advocate, thine eyes of mercy towards us." Look upon my miseries, and have pity on me.

THIRD POINT

In conclusion, to obtain eternal salvation the soul must be found at the last judgment having led a life conformable to the life of Jesus Christ: "Whom he foreknew he also predestinated to be made conformable to the image of His Son." (*Rom.* 8:29). It was this that caused Job to tremble: "What shall I do when God shall rise to judge me? And when he shall examine, what shall I answer him?" (*Job* 31:14). Philip II, rebuking a servant who had told him a lie, said: "Is it thus that thou deceivest me?" The unhappy man returned home, and died of grief. What will the sinner do? What can he answer to Jesus Christ, his Judge? He will, like the man in the Gospel who came to the feast without the wedding-garment, remain silent, not knowing what to answer: "But he was silent." (*Matt.* 12:12). His very sins will close his mouth: "All iniquity shall stop his mouth." (*Psalms* 106:42). St. Basil says, that the sinner will then be more tormented even by shame than

by the fire of Hell itself. "The shame shall be more terrible than the fire."

Behold, finally, the Judge will pronounce the sentence; "Depart from Me, you cursed, into everlasting
fire." Oh, what a terrible thunder-clap will that sentence be! "How terribly will that peal of thunder
resound!" says the Carthusian. St. Anselm says: "He
who trembles not at such a thunder does not sleep,
but is dead." And Eusebius adds, that such will be the
terror of sinners on hearing the sentence pronounced,
that were it possible they would die again: "Such terror will seize the wicked when they shall behold the
Judge giving sentence, that were they not immortal
they would die again." There is no more time then for
prayer, says St. Thomas of Villanova; there are no more
intercessors to whom to have recourse: "There is no
place for prayer: no one is at hand to intercede, no
friend, no father." To whom, then, can they fly? To God
perhaps, whom they have so greatly despised? "Who
shall deliver thee? shall that God whom thou hast
despised?"[55] To the Saints? To Mary? No, for then "the
stars (that is, their holy advocates) shall fall from
heaven; and the moon (which is Mary) shall not give
her light." (*Matt.* 24:29). St. Augustine says: "Mary will
fly from the gate of paradise."[56]

O God, exclaims St. Thomas of Villanova, with what
indifference do we hear the judgment spoken of! As if
the sentence of condemnation could not touch us, or
as if we were not to be judged: "Alas, with what security we speak and hear of these things! as if this sentence did not affect us, or as if that day would never
arrive."[57] And what folly, adds the same saint, to rest
secure in so perilous a matter! Say not, my brother,
St. Augustine admonishes thee, Ah, God will not surely
send me to Hell! Say it not, exclaims the saint; for the
Jews also could not persuade themselves that they
would be exterminated; so, many of the damned would
not believe that they would be sent to Hell; but still
the punishment came at last: "The end is come, the

end is come . . . now I will accomplish my anger in thee, and will judge thee." (*Ezech.* 7:6). And thus also, says St. Augustine, shall it happen to thee: "The day of judgment will come, and thou shalt find what God has threatened to be true." Now it rests with us to choose our own sentence. "Now it is in our own power what sentence we will have," says St. Eligius. What, then, must we do? Settle our accounts before the judgment: "Before judgment prepare thee justice." (Ecclus. 18:19). St. Bonaventure says, that to avoid failure, prudent merchants constantly look over and settle their accounts. "The judge may be appeased before judgment, but not during judgment," says St. Augustine. Let us, then, with St. Bernard, say to the Lord: "I desire to present myself before Thee already judged, and not to be judged." My Judge, I desire to be judged and punished by Thee in life, now that it is the time for mercy, and that Thou canst pardon me; for after death it will be the time for justice.

AFFECTIONS AND PRAYERS

My God, if I do not appease Thee now, there will then no longer be time for appeasing Thee. But how shall I appease Thee—I who have so often despised Thy friendship for miserable and brutal pleasures? I have repaid with ingratitude Thy immense love. What worthy satisfaction can a creature ever make for offenses committed against his Creator? Ah, my Lord, I thank Thee for having given me in Thy mercy the means of appeasing and satisfying Thy justice. I offer Thee the Blood and the death of Jesus Thy Son; and behold I already see Thy justice appeased, and superabundantly satisfied. For this my repentance is likewise necessary. Yes, my God, I repent with my whole heart of all the injuries I have done Thee. Judge me now, then, my Redeemer. I detest above every evil all the displeasure I have given Thee. I love Thee above all things with my whole heart; and I purpose always to love Thee, and rather to die than offend Thee anymore. Thou hast promised to pardon whosoever repents; ah, judge me then, now, and absolve me from my sins. I accept the punishment I deserve; but restore me to Thy grace, and preserve me in it till I die. Thus do I hope. O Mary, my Mother, I thank thee for the many mercies thou hast obtained for me; ah, continue to protect me to the end.

CONSIDERATION XV

On the General Judgment

"The Lord shall be known when He executeth judgments."   Psalms 9:11

FIRST POINT

At present, if we consider it well, there is no one more despised than Jesus Christ. We make more account of a peasant than of God; because if we insult a peasant, we fear that, being offended beyond endurance, he may avenge himself; but as for God, we insult Him, and heap insults freely on Him, as if He could not avenge Himself when He would: "They looked upon the Almighty as if He could do nothing." (*Job* 22:17). The Redeemer, therefore, has appointed a day, which will be the day of the general judgment (called emphatically in the Scriptures "the day of the Lord"), in which Jesus Christ will make Himself known as the all-powerful Lord which He is: "The Lord shall be known when He executeth judgments." (*Psalms* 9:17). Hence that day is no more called the day of mercy and of pardon, but the "day of wrath, a day of tribulation and distress, a day of calamity and misery." (*Soph.* 1:15). Yes, because the Lord will then justly redeem the honor which sinners have endeavored to rob Him of in this world. Let us consider how the judgment of that great day will take place.

Before the coming of the Judge "a fire shall go before Him." (*Psalms* 96:3). Fire will come down from Heaven, which will burn the earth and all the things of this earth: "The earth and the works that are in it shall he burnt up." (2 *Peter* 3:10). So that churches, palaces, villages, cities, kingdoms, all will become a heap of ashes. This house, corrupted by sin, must be purged by fire. Behold the end to which all the riches, pomps, and pleasures of this earth must come. When all men are dead, the trumpet shall sound, and all will rise: "The trumpet shall sound, and the dead shall rise." (1 *Cor.* 15:52). St. Jerome exclaimed: "I tremble whenever I consider the day of judgment: I seem always to hear that trumpet sounding in my ears—'Arise, ye dead, and come to judgment.'"[58] At the sound of this trumpet the beauteous souls of the just will descend to unite themselves to the bodies with which they have served God in this life; and the unhappy souls of the damned will come up from Hell to unite themselves to those accursed bodies with which they have offended God.

Oh, what a difference will there then be between the bodies of the just and those of the damned! The just will appear beautiful, fair, more resplendent than the sun: "Then shall the just shine as the sun." (*Matt.* 13:43). Happy he who in this life knows how to mortify his flesh by refusing it forbidden pleasures; and who, to keep it more in check, denies it even the lawful pleasures of the senses, and ill-treats it as the saints have done, Oh, how will he then rejoice, like St. Peter of Alcantara, who after his death said to St. Teresa: "O happy penance, which has merited for me so much glory!" On the other hand, the bodies of the reprobate will appear deformed, black, and stinking. Oh, what torment will it then be to the damned to be united to their bodies! Accursed body, the soul will say, to gratify thee I am lost. And the body will say: Accursed soul; and thou, who hadst the use of reason, why didst thou allow me those pleasures which have damned both thyself and me for all eternity?

AFFECTIONS AND PRAYERS

Ah, my Jesus and my Redeemer, who one day wilt be my Judge, pardon me before that day arrives. "Turn not away Thy face from me." Now Thou art a Father to me; and as a father receive into Thy favor a child who returns repentant to Thy feet. My Father, I ask pardon of Thee. I have offended Thee unjustly, I have left Thee unjustly. Thou didst not deserve such treatment from me. I repent of it, I grieve with my whole heart; pardon me, do not turn away from me, do not banish me as I deserve. Remember the Blood which Thou hast shed for me, and have pity on me. My Jesus. I wish for no other judge but Thee. St. Thomas of Villanova said: "I willingly submit to be judged by Him who died for me; and who, that I might not be condemned, chose to be Himself condemned to the cross." And St. Paul had said the same before him: "Who is He that shall condemn? Christ Jesus, that died for us." (*Rom.* 8:34). My Father, I love "Thee; and in future I will never again leave Thy feet. Forget my offenses against Thee, and give me a great love for Thy goodness. I desire to love Thee more than I have offended Thee; but without Thy aid I cannot love Thee. Assist me, my Jesus, make me live grateful to Thy love, that on the last day I may be found in the valley amongst the number of Thy lovers. O Mary, my Queen and my Advocate, assist me now; for if I am lost, in that day thou wilt be able no longer to assist me. Thou prayest for all; pray also for me, who glory in being thy devoted servant, and confide so much in thee.

SECOND POINT

When all men shall have arisen, they shall be told by the angels to go to the Valley of Josaphat, there to be judged: "Nations, nations, in the valley of destruction: for the day of the Lord is near." (*Joel* 3:14). As soon as they are assembled, the angels will come and separate the reprobate from the elect: "The angels shall go out and separate the wicked from among the just." (*Matt.* 13:49). The just shall be at the right, and the wicked be driven to the left. How great would be the pain of anyone to find himself banished from society, or expelled from the Church! But how much greater will be the pain of being banished from the society of the saints! "How will the wicked be confounded when, separated from the just, they find themselves abandoned!"[59] St. Chrysostom says, "that if the damned had no other pain, this confusion alone would be enough to constitute their Hell."[60] The son shall be separated from the father, the husband from the wife, the master from the servant: "One shall be taken, and the other shall be left." (*Matt.* 24:40). Tell me, my brother, which place, think you, will fall to your lot! Would you wish to be found at the right? Quit, then, the life that leads you to the left.

In this world the great and the rich are considered fortunate; and the saints, who live in poverty and humiliation, are despised. Oh, ye faithful souls who love God, be not troubled at finding yourselves despised and afflicted on this earth: "Your sorrow shall be turned into joy." (*John* 16:20). Then shall you be called truly fortunate, and have the honor of being declared to belong to the court of Jesus Christ. Oh, how great will then appear St. Peter of Alcantara, who was despised as if he were an apostate! St. John of God, who was treated as a madman! St. Peter Celestine, who, having renounced the papal throne, died in a prison! Oh, what honors will then be bestowed on so many martyrs who were tormented by their executioners! "Then shall every man have praise from God." (*1 Cor.* 4:5). And oh, how horrible will Herod, Pilate, Nero appear, and so many other great ones of the earth, but condemned to Hell! O lovers of the world, in the valley, in the valley, I expect you. There you will doubtless change your opinions. There you will weep over your folly. Miserable ones, who for the sake of making a figure for a short time on the theatre of this world, will hereafter have to act the part of reprobates in the tragedy of the judgment. The elect shall then be placed on the right; nay, according to the Apostle, they shall, for their greater glory, be raised in the air above the clouds, to go with the angels to meet Jesus Christ, who will descend from Heaven: "We shall be caught up together with them in the clouds to meet Christ in the air." (*1 Thess.* 4:16). And the damned, like so many goats destined for slaughter, shall be confined on the left to await their Judge, who will pronounce the public condemnation of all His enemies.

But behold the heavens open, and the angels come to assist at the judgment, carrying, according to St. Thomas, the symbols of the passion of Jesus Christ: "When the Lord comes to judgment, the sign of the cross, and the other symbols of the passion, shall be seen:"[61] The cross especially shall appear: "And then shall appear the sign of the son of man in heaven, and then shall all the tribes of the earth mourn." (*Matt.* 24:30). Cornelius à Lapide says: "Oh, how then, at the sight of the cross, shall sinners weep, who during life made no account of their eternal salvation, which cost the Son of God so much!" Then, says St. Chrysostom, "the nails will complain of thee, the wounds will speak against thee, the cross of Christ will preach against thee."[62] The holy Apostles and all their imitators will also assist as assessors at this judgment, and, together with Jesus Christ, will judge the nations: "The just shall shine, they shall judge the nations." (*Wis.* 3:7, 8), Mary, the Queen of Saints and Angels, will come to assist; and finally, the Eternal Judge will come seated on a throne of majesty and light: "And they shall see the son of man coming in the clouds of heaven with much power and majesty." (*Matt.* 24:40): "At their presence the people shall be in grievous pains." (*Joel* 2:6). The light of Jesus Christ will console the elect; but to the reprobate it will be a greater torment than Hell itself.

St. Jerome says: "It were easier for the damned to bear the pains of Hell than the presence of the Lord." St. Teresa said: "My Jesus, afflict me with every pain; but do not let me behold Thy countenance enraged against me on that day." And St. Basil: "This confusion surpasses all pains." Then will happen what St. John foretold, that the damned will call upon the mountains to fall upon them, and to hide them from the sight of their angry Judge: "They say to the mountains and to the rocks: Fall upon us, and hide us from the face of Him that sitteth upon the throne and from the Lamb." (*Apoc.* 4:16).

AFFECTIONS AND PRAYERS

O my dear Redeemer, O Lamb of God, who camest into the world, not to punish, but to pardon sins—ah, pardon me speedily, before that day comes in which Thou wilt have to judge me. Then the sight of the Lamb, who has borne with me with so much patience, would be to me the Hell of Hells should I perchance be lost. Again I say, Ah, pardon me speedily; draw me by Thy merciful Hand from the precipice into which I have fallen through my sins. I repeat, O Sovereign Good, of having offended Thee, and so greatly offended Thee. I love Thee, O my Judge, who hast so much loved me. Ah, through the merits of Thy death give me a great grace, that may change me from a sinner into a saint. Thou hast promised to hear those who pray to Thee: "Cry to me, and I will hear thee." (*Jer.* 33:3). I do not ask for earthly goods; I ask for Thy grace, Thy love, and nothing else. Hear me, my Jesus, by that love which Thou didst bear me in dying for me upon the cross. My beloved Judge, I am a criminal; but a criminal who loves Thee more than himself. Have pity on me. Mary, my Mother, make haste, make haste to aid me now that there is time for thee to aid me. Thou hast not abandoned me when I lived forgetful of thee and of God; help me now that I am resolved to serve

thee always, and never more to offend my Lord. O
Mary, thou art my hope.

THIRD POINT

But behold the judgment now commences. The books
are opened; that is, the conscience of each one: "The
judgment sat, and the books were opened." (*Dan.* 7:10).
The witnesses against the reprobate shall be, first, the
devils, who will say, according to St. Augustine: "Most
just Judge, declare him to be ours who would not be
Thine." Secondly, their own conscience: "Their conscience
bearing witness to them." (*Rom.* 2:15). Moreover the
very walls of the house in which they have offended
God shall bear witness against them, and shall cry for
vengeance: "The stones shall cry out of the wall."
(*Hab.* 2:11). Finally, the Judge Himself, who has been
present at all the offenses committed against Him,
shall be a witness: "I am the Judge and the witness,
saith the Lord." (*Jer.* 29:23). St. Paul says, that the
Lord will then "bring to light the hidden things of
darkness." (*1 Cor.* 4:5). He will make known to all men
the most secret and shameful sins of the reprobate,
which in their lifetime have been concealed even from
their confessors: "I will discover thy shame to thy face."
(*Nahum* 3:5). The Master of the Sentences, as well as
others, is of opinion that the sins of the elect will not
be manifested, but be concealed; according to the words
of David: "Blessed are they whose iniquities are forgiven, and whose sins are covered." (*Psalms* 31:1). On
the other hand, says St. Basil, "the sins of the reprobate shall be seen by all at a glance, as in a picture."[63]
St. Thomas says: If in the garden of Gethsemani, when
Jesus Christ said, "*Ego sum*" (I am He), all the sol-
diers who came to seize Him fell prostrate to the ground,
what will the damned feel when, seated as Judge, He
shall say to them: Behold, I am He whom you have so
greatly despised "What will He do when about to judge,
who did this when about to be judged?"[64]

But let us proceed. Now comes the sentence. Jesus Christ will first turn to the elect, and address to them those consoling words: "Come, ye blessed of my father, possess the kingdom prepared for you from the foundation of the world." (*Matt.* 25:34). When it was revealed to St. Francis of Assisi that he was amongst the elect, he was beside himself with joy. What joy will it be, then, to hear the Judge say, Come, ye blessed children, come to the kingdom prepared for you; for you there are no more pains, no more fears; you are and shall be safe forever. I bless the Blood which I shed for you; and I bless the tears you have shed for your sins: let us ascend to paradise, where we shall be together for all eternity. Mary will also bless her servants, and invite them to accompany her to Heaven; and thus, singing *Alleluia, Alleluia,* the elect will enter Heaven in triumph, to possess, to praise, and love God forever and ever.

On the other hand, the reprobate, turning to Jesus Christ, will say to Him: "And we wretches, what will become of us?" The eternal Judge will say: As for you, since you have renounced and despised My grace, "depart from me, you cursed, into everlasting fire." (*Matt.* 25:41). Depart from Me, for I will neither see nor hear you anymore. Go; and go with My curse upon you, since you have despised My blessing. And where, O Lord are these miserable wretches to go? "Into the fire." To Hell, to burn both body and soul. And for how many years, or for how many ages? Years! Ages! "Into everlasting fire." For all eternity, as long as God shall be God. After this sentence, the reprobate, says St. Ephrem, shall bid farewell to the angels, the saints, their relations, and to the Divine Mother: "Farewell, ye just; farewell, O Cross; farewell, Heaven. Farewell, fathers and children, since we shall never more behold you. Farewell also, O Mary, Mother of God."[65] And thus in the midst of the valley a great pit will be opened, into which the devils and the damned shall fall together; and they shall hear—O God!—those gates close after them which will never more be opened, never, never, for all eternity. O accursed sin, to what a miserable end wilt thou one day conduct so many poor souls! O unhappy souls, for whom this lamentable end is reserved!

AFFECTIONS AND PRAYERS

Ah, my Saviour and my God, what will my sentence be on that day? If now, my Jesus, Thou wert to demand of me an account of my life, what could I reply to Thee, but that I deserved a thousand Hells? Yes, it is true, my dear Redeemer, I deserve a thousand Hells: but know that I love Thee, and love Thee more than myself; and as for the offenses I have committed against Thee, I feel so great a sorrow for them, that I should be content rather to have suffered every evil than to have offended Thee. O my Jesus, Thou condemnest obstinate sinners, but not those who repent and wish to love Thee. Behold me repentant at Thy feet; make me feel that Thou pardonest me. But Thou dost already make me feel it by the words of Thy Prophet: "Turn ye to me, and I will turn to you." (*Zach.* 1:3). I leave all, I renounce all the pleasures and riches of the world; and turn to Thee, and embrace Thee, my beloved Redeemer. Ah, receive me into Thy Heart, and there inflame me with Thy holy love; inflame me so that I may never again think of separating myself from Thee. My Jesus, save me; and may my salvation be to love Thee always, and always to praise Thy mercies. "The mercies of the Lord I will sing forever." Mary, my hope, my refuge, and my Mother, aid me, and obtain for me holy perseverance. No one ever was lost who had recourse to thee. I commend myself to thee; have pity on me.

CONSIDERATION XVI

On the Pains of Hell

"And these shall go into everlasting pun-
ishment."   Matthew 25:46

FIRST POINT

The sinner commits two evils when he sins; he leaves God, his sovereign good, and he turns to creatures: "For my people have done two evils: they have forsaken me, the fountain of living water, and have digged to themselves cisterns, broken cisterns, that can hold no water." (*Jer.* 2:13). Because, then, the sinner turns to creatures, with an aversion to God, he shall be justly tormented in Hell by those very creatures, by fire and by the devils; and this is the pain of sense. But because his greatest guilt, and that in which sin consists, is the turning away from God, therefore the principal torment, and which will constitute Hell, will be the pain of loss, that is, the pain of having lost God.

Let us consider first the pain of sense. It is of faith that there is a Hell. In the middle of the earth is this prison, reserved for the punishment of those who rebel against God. What is this Hell? It is a place of torments; thus was Hell called by the glutton who was damned (*Luke* 16:28): a place of torments where all the senses and the powers of the damned shall have their appropriate torment; and the more a person has offended God in any particular sense, so much the more shall he be tormented in that sense: "By what things a man sinneth, by the same also he is tormented." (*Wis.* 11:17): "As much as she hath been in delicacies, so much torment and sorrow give unto her." (*Apoc.* 18:7). The sight shall be tormented with darkness: "A land that is dark and covered with the mist of death." (*Job* 10:21). With what compassion should we hear that a poor man was enclosed in a dark pit for his whole life, or for forty or fifty years! Hell is a pit enclosed on every side, where no ray of the sun or any other light ever enters: "He shall never see light." (*Psalms* 48:20). Fire, which on earth gives light, in Hell shall be dark: "The voice of the Lord which divides the flame from the fire." (*Psalms* 28:7). St. Basil explains it: "The Lord will divide the fire from the light, so that this fire will only perform the office of burning, and not of giving light." And still more briefly does Albertus Magnus explain it: "He will divide the splendor from the heat." The same smoke that issues from this fire will form that storm of darkness of which St. Jude speaks, which will blind the eyes of the damned: "To whom the storm of darkness is reserved forever." (*Jude* 13). St. Thomas says, that there will only be sufficient light allowed to the damned to torment them the more: "Just sufficient to see those things which can torment them."[66] In that twilight they will behold the hideousness of the other reprobates and of the devils, who will assume horrible forms to terrify them the more.

The sense of smell shall be tormented. What torment would it be to find oneself shut up in a room with a putrid corpse! "Out of their carcases shall rise a stink." (Isaias 34:3). The damned must remain in the midst of so many millions of other reprobates, who are alive to pain, but corpses as to the stench they send forth. St. Bonaventure says, that if the body of one of the damned were driven from Hell, the stench would be enough to destroy all men. And yet some fools say: If I go to Hell, I shall not be alone. Miserable beings! The more there are in Hell, the more they suffer: "There (says St. Thomas) the society of the wretched will not diminish, but rather increase, the wretchedness."[67] They suffer more, I say, from the smell, the shrieks, and the narrowness of the place; besides which, in Hell they will be one over another, heaped up together like sheep in the winter season: "They are laid in hell like sheep." (*Psalms* 48:15). Nay more, they will be like grapes crushed under the press of the wrath of God: "He treadeth the wine-press of the fury of the wrath of God the Almighty." (*Apoc.* 19:15). From this also shall come the pain of immobility: "Let them become immovable as a stone." (*Ex.* 15:16). Thus, as the damned fall into Hell at the last day, so will they have to remain, without ever changing their position, and without moving hand or foot, as long as God is God.

The hearing shall be tormented by the continual howling and wailing of those despairing wretches. The devils will make perpetual noises: "The sound of dread is always in his ears." (*Job* 15:21). How painful is it to one who wishes to sleep, to hear the continual moaning of a sick person, the barking of a dog, or the crying of a child! Unhappy souls, who are condemned to hear continually for all eternity the cries and howls of those tortured wretches! The appetite shall be tormented by hunger: the damned shall suffer from a ravenous hunger: "They shall suffer hunger as dogs." (*Psalms* 58:15); but never shall they taste even a crumb of bread. So great will be their thirst, that the water of the ocean would not suffice to quench it; and yet never shall they obtain even a drop of water. The glutton asked for one single drop; but never yet has he obtained it, and never, never shall he have it.

AFFECTIONS AND PRAYERS

All, my Lord, behold at Thy feet one who has made but small account of Thy grace and Thy punishments. Unhappy me; if Thou, my Jesus, hadst not taken pity upon me, how many years should I now have been in that stinking furnace, where so many like myself are already burning! Ah, my Redeemer, how is it that, reflecting upon this, I do not burn with Thy love? How can I in future ever think of offending Thee again? Ah, may it never be, my Jesus! Let me rather die a thousand times. Since Thou hast begun, complete the work. Thou hast delivered me from the mire of my many sins, and with so much love hast called me to love

Thee. Ah, grant now that I may spend wholly for Thee all the time Thou givest me. How would the damned desire one day, one hour of the time which Thou grantest me! And what, then, shall I do? Shall I continue to spend it in displeasing Thee? No, my Jesus, do not permit it, by the merits of that Blood which has hitherto delivered me from Hell. I love Thee, O my Sovereign Good; and because I love Thee, I repent of having offended Thee. I will offend Thee no more, but always love Thee. My Queen and my Mother Mary, pray to Jesus for me; and obtain for me the gift of perseverance and of His holy love.

SECOND POINT

The most cruel suffering to the senses of the damned is the fire of Hell, which torments the touch: "The vengeance on the flesh of the ungodly is fire and worms." (*Ecclus.* 7:19). Hence the Lord in the judgment makes special mention of it: "Depart from me, you cursed, into everlasting fire." (*Matt.* 25:41). Even in this life the pain of fire is the greatest of all pains; but the difference between our fire and that of Hell is such, that, according to St. Augustine, ours appears but as painted fire: "In comparison of which our fire here is as painted fire." And St. Vincent Ferrer says, that in comparison with it our fire is cold. The reason of this is, because our fire is created for our use; but the fire of Hell is created by God expressly to torment, "Fire," says Tertullian, "which is made for the use of man in this world, is very different from that which is used for the justice of God." The wrath of God lights up this avenging fire: "A fire is kindled in my rage." (*Jer.* 15:14). Hence the prophet Isaias calls the fire of Hell the spirit of heat: "If the Lord shall wash away the filth . . . by the spirit of burning." (*Isaias* 4:4). The damned shall be sent not *to* the fire, but *into* the fire: "Depart from Me, you cursed, *into* everlasting fire." So that the unhappy wretch will be surrounded by fire like wood in a furnace. He will find an abyss of fire below, an abyss above, and an abyss on every side. If he touches, if he sees, if he breathes, he touches, he sees, he breathes only fire. He will be in fire like a fish in water. This fire will not only surround the damned, but it will enter into his bowels to torment him. His body will become all fire; so that the bowels within him will burn, his heart will burn in his bosom, his brains in his head, his blood in his veins, even the marrow in his bones: each reprobate will in himself become a furnace of fire: "Thou shalt make them as an oven of fire." (*Psalms* 20:10).

Some cannot bear to walk on a road burnt up by the sun, to remain in a close room with a brasier, nor can they endure a spark that flies from a candle; and yet they fear not that fire which devours, as Isaias says: "Which of you can dwell with devouring fire?" (*Isaias* 33:14). As a wild-beast devours a kid, so the fire of Hell devours the damned; it devours without ever destroying him. Continue, O fool, says St. Peter Damian (speaking to the unchaste), continue to gratify thy flesh; for the day will come in which thy impurities will become as pitch in thy entrails, to increase and aggravate the torments of the flame which will burn thee in Hell: "The day will come, yea rather the night, when thy lust shall be turned into pitch, to feed in thy bowels the everlasting fire."[68] St. Jerome adds, that that fire will bring with it all the torments and pains which we suffer from on this earth; pains in the side, in the head, the bowels, the nerves: "In this one fire the sinners in Hell endure all torments." In this fire there will even be the pain of cold: "Let him pass from the snow waters to excessive heat." (*Job* 24:19). But we must ever bear in mind that all the pains of this earth are but a shadow according to St. Chrysostom, in comparison of the pains of Hell: "Imagine fire, imagine the knife; what are these but a shadow compared with those torments!" The powers of the soul will also have their appropriate torment. The damned will be tormented in his memory, by the remembrance of the time which was given him in this life to save his soul, and which he spent in losing it; and of the graces which he received from God, and of which he did not profit. He will be tormented in the understanding by recalling the great good which he has lost— Heaven and God; and that this loss can never be repaired. In the will, by perceiving that whatever he asks shall always be denied him: "The desire of the sinner shall perish." (*Psalms* 111:10). The unhappy wretch will never have anything he desires, and always have all that he abhors, which will be his eternal sufferings. He would wish to escape from his torments, and to find peace; but he will always be tormented, and never shall find peace.

AFFECTIONS AND PRAYERS

Ah, my Jesus, Thy blood and Thy death are my hope. Thou hast died to deliver me from eternal death. Ah, my Lord, and who has participated more in the merits of Thy passion than I, wretch that I am, who have so often deserved Hell? Ah, let me no longer live ungrateful for the many graces Thou hast bestowed on me. Thou hast delivered me from the fire of Hell, because Thou desirest not that I should burn in that fire of torment, but with the sweet fire of Thy love. Assist me, then, that I may comply with Thy desire. Were I now in Hell, I could never more love Thee; but since I am able to love Thee, I will love Thee, I love Thee, O Infinite Goodness; I love Thee, my Redeemer, who hast so much loved me. How have I been able to live so long forgetful of Thee! I thank Thee for not having forgotten me. If Thou hadst forgotten me, I should either now have been in Hell, or I should have had no sorrow for my sins. This sorrow for having offended Thee which I feel in my heart, and this desire which I experience to love Thee much, are gifts of Thy grace, which still assists me. I thank Thee, my Jesus. I hope in future to dedicate to Thee the remainder of my life. I renounce all. I will think only of serving and pleasing Thee. Recall to me at all times the Hell that I have merited, and the graces Thou hast bestowed on me; and permit not that I should again turn my back on Thee, and condemn myself to that pit of torments. O Mother of God, pray for me a sinner. Thy intercession has delivered me from Hell; let it again preserve me, my Mother, from sin, which alone can condemn me afresh to Hell.

THIRD POINT

But all these pains are as nothing in comparison with the pain of loss. It is not the darkness, nor the stench, nor the cries, nor the fire, that makes Hell; the pain that makes Hell is the pain of having lost God. St. Bruno says: "Let torments be added to torments, as long as they are not deprived of God."[69] And St. John Chrysostom: "If thou namest a thousand Hells, thou wilt have said nothing that can compare to such a pain."[70] And St. Augustine adds, that if the damned could enjoy the sight of God "they would feel no pain, and Hell itself would be changed into paradise:"[71] To form some idea of this pain, consider that if (for example) a person loses a gem worth a hundred crowns, he feels great pain; but if it be worth two hundred, he feels double pain; if four hundred, still more: in a word, the greater the value of the thing lost, the greater the pain. Now what is the good the damned have lost? They have lost God, who is an infinite good; hence, says St. Thomas, their pain is in a certain manner infinite: "The pain of the damned is infinite, because it is the loss of an infinite good."[72]

This is the only pain dreaded by the saints. St. Augustine says: "This is the pain for those who love, not for those who despise." St. Ignatius Loyola said: "Lord, I can endure every pain; but to be deprived of Thee, no, this I cannot bear." But this pain is in no way feared

by sinners, who are content to live months and years
without God, because, unhappy that they are, they live
in the midst of darkness. In death, however, they will
discover the great good which they lose. The soul, in
quitting this life, instantly comprehends that she has
been created for God, according to St. Antoninus: "As
soon as the soul is separated from the body she under-
stands that God is the sovereign good, and that she
was created for Him." Hence she suddenly rushes forward to embrace her sovereign good; but being in sin,
God banishes her from Him. If a dog sees a hare, and
is withheld by a chain, how it struggles to break the
chain, and to go and seize the prey! The soul, in leaving the body, is naturally drawn to God; but sin sep-
arates it from God, and sends it far away to Hell: "Your
iniquities have divided between you and your God."
(*Isaias* 59:2). Hell, then, consists entirely in that first
word of the condemnation, "Depart from Me, you
cursed." Go, Jesus Christ will say; never shall you again
behold My face. "A thousand Hells cannot be compared
to the pain of being hateful to Christ."[73] When David
condemned Absalom never again to appear before him,
so great was this punishment to Absalom that he
replied: "Tell my father either to permit me to see his
face, or to kill me." (*2 Kings* 14:32). Philip the Second
said to a nobleman whose behavior he observed to be
irreverent in church: "Never more appear in my presence." So great was the affliction of that nobleman,
that on his return home he died of grief. What, then,
will it be when God says to the reprobate: Depart, I
will never see thee more? "I will hide my face from
them, and all evils and afflictions shall find them."
(*Deut.* 31:17). You (Jesus Christ will say to the reprobate at the last day) are no longer Mine; I am no longer
yours: "Call his name, not my people; for you are not
my people, and I will not be yours." (*Osee* 1:9). What
a grief is it to a son who loses a father, or to a wife
who loses a husband, to say: My father (or my husband), I shall see thee no more! Ah, if we could now

hear the lamentations of a lost soul, and were to ask: Soul, why weepest thou so much? its only answer would be: I weep because I have lost God, and shall never see Him more. If at least the miserable soul could love its God in Hell, and resign itself to His will! But no; could it do this, Hell would not be Hell; the unhappy soul cannot resign itself to the will of God, because it has become an enemy to the divine will. Neither can it any more love its God; but it hates Him, and will forever hate Him; and this will be its Hell, to know that God is a supreme good, and to find itself constrained to hate Him at the same time that it knows Him to be worthy of infinite love. "I am that perfidious one deprived of the love of God," such was the reply of that devil interrogated by St. Catherine of Genoa as to who he was. The damned will hate and curse God; and cursing God, they will also curse the benefits He has bestowed on them—their creation, redemption, the Sacraments, and especially those of baptism, penance, and, above all, the most holy Sacrament of the altar. They will hate all the angels and saints, but especially their guardian angels, and their holy advocates; and more than all, the Divine Mother. But principally will they curse the three Divine Persons; and of these, especially the Son of God, who once died for their salvation; they will curse His wounds, His blood, His pains, and His death.

AFFECTIONS AND PRAYERS

Ah, my God, Thou art, then, my Sovereign Good, Infinite Good; and I have so often voluntarily lost Thee! I well knew that by my sin I caused Thee great displeasure, and that I lost Thy grace; and yet I committed it. Ah, if I did not see Thee nailed to the cross, O Son of God, dying for me, I should no longer have courage to ask and to hope for Thy pardon. Eternal Father, look not upon me, look upon this beloved Son, who implores of Thee mercy for me; hear Him, and pardon me. I ought now for years past to have been in Hell, without any hope of ever again being able to love Thee, and to recover Thy lost grace. My God, I grieve above all other evils for this injury I have done Thee, of renouncing Thy friendship, and despising Thy love, for the miserable pleasures of this earth. Oh, that I had rather died a thousand times! How can I have been so blind and so mad! I thank Thee, my Lord, for giving me time to repair the evil I have done. Since by Thy mercy I am not in Hell, and can still love Thee, my God, I will love Thee. I will no longer defer my entire conversion to Thee. I love Thee, O Infinite Goodness; I love Thee, my life, my treasure, my love, my all. Ever recall to me, O Lord, the love Thou hast borne me, and the Hell where I ought now to be, in order that this thought may always inflame me to make acts of the love of Thee, and to say always to Thee, I love Thee, I love Thee, I love Thee. O Mary, my Queen, my Hope, and my Mother, if I were in Hell I could not love thee either anymore. I love thee, my Mother; and I trust in thee never again to cease to love thee and my God. Aid me; pray to Jesus for me.

CONSIDERATION XVII

On the Eternity of Hell

"And these shall go into everlasting punishment."   Mark 25:40

FIRST POINT

If Hell were not eternal, it would not be Hell. That pain which does not last long is not a great pain. One person submits to have a cancer cut away, another to have a gangrene cauterized; the pain is severe, but as it is soon over, the suffering is not much. How great, however, would be the agony, if that incision, or that operation of cauterizing, were to last for a week, or for a whole month! When the pain lasts long, even though it be slight, as a pain in the eyes, or a swelling, it becomes insupportable. But why talk of pain? Even a play, or a concert, that lasts too long, were it for an entire day, would be unendurably tedious. And if it should last a month, a year? What, then, will Hell be? There is no question there of hearing always the same play, or the same music; none of a mere pain in the eyes, a swelling only; none of the torture of an incision, or of a red-hot iron: but of all torments, all sufferings. And for how long? For all eternity: "And they shall be tormented day and night for ever and ever." (*Apoc.* 20:10).

This eternity is of faith; it is not a simple opinion, but a truth attested by God in so many places in the Scriptures: "Depart from me, you cursed, into everlasting fire." "And these shall go into everlasting punishment." "Who shall suffer eternal punishment in destruction." "Every one shall be salted with fire." (*Matt.* 25:41; *Ibid.* 46; *2 Thess.* 1:9; *Mark* 9:48). As salt preserves things, so the fire of Hell, whilst it torments the damned, acts as salt by preserving their lives. "There fire consumes," says St. Bernard, "that it may always preserve."[74]

What madness would it be in a man, who, in order to enjoy one day of amusement, should condemn himself to be shut up in a pit for twenty or thirty years! If Hell were to last a hundred years, nay, only two or three years, still it would be a great folly to condemn himself for a moment of vile pleasure to two or three years of fire. But it is not a question of thirty, of a hundred, of a thousand, nor of a hundred thousand years; it is a question of eternity, of suffering forever the same torments, which will never end, nor be alleviated for a moment. The Saints, then, had reason to weep and tremble whilst they were in this life, and still in danger of being lost. The blessed Isaias also, though living in the desert amidst fasting and penance, wept, saying: "Unhappy me, for I am not yet free from the danger of hellfire."

AFFECTIONS AND PRAYERS

Ah, my God, if Thou hadst sent me to Hell, as I have oftentimes deserved, and hadst afterwards in Thy mercy delivered me from it, how great would my obligations have been to Thee! And from that time what a holy life should I have begun to lead! And now that, with still greater mercy, Thou hast preserved me from falling into it, what shall I do? Shall I again offend Thee, and provoke Thee to anger, in order that Thou mayest precisely send me to burn in that prison of rebels, where so many are already burning for less sins than mine? Ah, my Redeemer, thus have I acted in the past; instead of making use of the time Thou gavest me that I might weep for my sins, I have spent it in provoking Thee still more. I thank Thy infinite goodness for having borne with me so long. Were it not infinite, how could it have endured me? I thank Thee, then, for having waited for me till now with so much patience; and I thank Thee most especially for the light Thou now givest me, by which Thou makest me perceive my folly, and the wrong I have done Thee in insulting Thee by my many sins. My Jesus, I detest them, and I repent of them with all my heart; pardon me through Thy Passion, and assist me by Thy grace, that I may never more offend Thee. I may now justly fear that if I commit another mortal sin, Thou wilt abandon me. Ah, my Lord, I beseech Thee, place before my eyes this just fear whenever the devil shall again tempt me to offend Thee. My God, I love Thee, nor will I lose Thee any more; assist me by Thy grace. Aid me, O most holy Virgin; grant that I may always have recourse to thee in my temptations, that I may never again lose my God. Mary, thou art my hope.

SECOND POINT

Whoever once enters Hell shall never quit it more for all eternity. This thought caused David to tremble, saying: "Let not the deep swallow me up, and let not the pit shut her mouth upon me." (*Psalms* 68:16). The damned once fallen into that pit of torments, its mouth is closed, never again to be opened. In Hell there is a gate to enter in at, but there is none by which to go out: "There shall be a way to descend," says Eusebius Emissenus, "but none to ascend." And he thus explains the words of the Psalmist: "Let not the pit shut her mouth, because after having received the reprobate, it will be closed above and opened below." As long as the sinner lives, he can always hope for a remedy; but once overtaken by death in sin, all hope will be ended for him: "When the wicked man is dead, there shall be no hope any more." (*Prov.* 11:7). If at least the damned could flatter themselves with false hopes, and thus find some alleviation to their despair! That poor wounded man confined to his bed, and despaired of by the physician, still flatters and comforts himself, saying: "Who knows but I may yet find some physician and some remedy that may heal me?" That poor wretch condemned to the galleys for life, also consoles himself, saying: "Who knows what may happen, and I may free myself from these chains?" If (I say) the damned could at least speak thus also: "Who knows but I may one day escape from this prison?" and could thus delude themselves with this false hope! But no, in Hell there is no hope, neither true nor false; there is no *Who knows?* The unhappy wretch will always have written before his eyes his condemnation, to weep forever in that pit of torments: "Some unto life everlasting, and others unto reproach, to see it always." (*Dan.* 12:2). Hence the damned not only suffer what they suffer in each moment, but they suffer in each moment the pain of eternity, saying: "What I now suffer I shall have to suffer forever." "They bear the weight of eternity," says Tertullian.

Let us, then, pray to the Lord, according to the prayer of St. Augustine: "Here burn, here cut, here do not spare, that Thou mayest spare in eternity!" The punishments of this life pass: "Thy arrows pass: the voice of thy thunder in a wheel." (*Psalms* 76:19). But the punishments of the other life never pass. Let us fear these; let us fear that thunder of eternal condemnation, which will issue from the mouth of the Judge, when He judges the reprobate: "Depart from Me, you cursed, into everlasting fire." He says, "in a wheel;" a wheel being a figure of eternity, to which there is no end: "I have drawn My sword out of its sheath, not to be turned back." (*Ezech.* 21:5). The punishment of Hell will be great; but that which ought most to terrify us is, that it will be irrevocable.

But what sort of justice is this, the unbeliever will exclaim, to punish a sin that lasts but a moment with eternal pain? But, I reply, how can a sinner have the courage to offend for a momentary pleasure a God of infinite majesty? Even by the rule of human justice (says St. Thomas), the punishment is not measured according to the duration of the time, but according to the nature of the crere: "Murder, because committed in a moment, is not therefore punished by a momentary pain."[75]

Hell is but little for a mortal sin. An offense against Infinite Majesty deserves an infinite punishment, says St. Bernardine of Sienna: "By every mortal sin an infinite injury is done to God; and to an infinite injury an infinite punishment is due." But because, says the angelical Doctor, the creature is not capable of infinite pain as to intensity, God justly ordains that it be infinite as to extension.

Moreover this pain must necessarily be eternal: first, because the damned can no longer satisfy for their sins. In this life the penitent sinner can satisfy for his sins in so far as the merits of Jesus Christ are applied to him; but the damned soul is excluded from these merits, so that not being able any more to appease God, and his sin being eternal, eternal also must be his punishment: "He shall not give to God his ransom, and shall labour for ever." (*Psalms* 48:8, 9). Hence Belluacensis says: "There sin can be forever punished, and never expiated;" since, according to St. Augustine, "there the sinner cannot repent;" therefore the Lord will be forever angry with him: "The people with whom the Lord is angry forever." (*Mal.* 1:4). Moreover, even though God should desire to pardon the damned, they will not be pardoned, because their will is obstinate, and confirmed in hatred against God. Innocent III says: "The reprobate will not humble themselves, but the malignity of hatred will go on always increasing in them."[76] And St. Jerome: "They are insatiable in the desire of sinning."[77] Therefore the wounds of the damned are desperate, since they refuse even to be healed: "His sorrow is become perpetual and the wound desperate, so as to refuse to be healed." (*Jer.* 15:18).

AFFECTIONS AND PRAYERS

So, then, my Redeemer, were I now in Hell, according to my deserts, I should obstinately hate Thee, my God, who hast died for me! O God, and what a Hell would this be to hate Thee, who hast loved me so much, and who art infinitely good, and worthy of infinite love! If I were now in Hell, I should also be in so unhappy a state that I should not even desire the pardon Thou now offerest me. My Jesus, I thank Thee for the mercy Thou hast shown me; and since I can now obtain pardon, and can love Thee, I wish to be pardoned, and I wish to love Thee. Thou offerest me pardon, and I ask it of Thee, and I hope for it through Thy merits. I repent of all my offenses against Thee, O Infinite Goodness, and do Thou pardon me. I love Thee with my whole soul. Ah, Lord, and what evil hast Thou done me, that I should hate Thee as my enemy forever. And what friend have I ever had, who has done and suffered for me what Thou hast, O my Jesus? Ah, do not permit me

again to incur Thy displeasure, and to forfeit Thy love;
rather let me die than allow this utter ruin to befall
me! O Mary, shelter me under the mantle of thy protection, and never let me depart from it, so that I should
again rebel against God and against thee!

THIRD POINT

Death in this life is feared above all things by sinners, but in Hell it will be above all desired: "They
shall seek death, and shall not find it; and they shall
desire to die, and death shall fly from them." (*Apoc.*
9:6). Hence St. Jerome said: "O death, how grateful
wouldst thou be to those to whom thou wert so bitter!"[78] David says that death shall feed upon the
damned. (*Psalms* 48:15). St. Bernard, in explaining this,
observes, that as the sheep, feeding upon grass, eats
the blades, and leaves the roots, so death feeds upon
the damned, kills them every moment, and yet leaves
them life, that it may continue to kill them by torments
for all eternity. So that, according to St. Gregory, the
damned die every moment, without ever dying: "Delivered up to the avenging flames, he will forever die." If
a man dies of pain, everyone compassionates him. Had
the damned at least but some one to compassionate
them! But no, the unhappy wretches die in each instant
of pain, and neither have, nor ever will have, anyone
to pity them. The Emperor Zeno being enclosed in a
dungeon, cried aloud: "Liberate me for mercy's sake."
No one heard him, and he was found dead, having died
in despair; for he had eat the very flesh off his arms.
The damned cry from the pit of Hell, says St. Cyril of
Alexandria, but no one comes to deliver them from it,
and no one compassionates them.

And how long will this their misery last? For ever
and ever. It is related in the Spiritual Exercises of
Father Segneri the younger (written by Muratori), that,
in Rome, the devil, who dwelt in one obsessed, being
asked how long he would have to remain in Hell, replied,

in a rage, beating his hand against a chair, "Forever, forever." So great was the terror thus inspired, that many youths of the Roman Seminary, who were there present, made a general confession, and changed their lives at this great sermon of two words—"forever, forever." Poor Judas! above seventeen hundred years have elapsed since he has been in Hell, and his Hell is still only beginning. Poor Cain! he has been burning in flames for above five thousand and seven hundred years, and his Hell is still but beginning. Another devil was asked, since when had he been in Hell; and he replied, "Yesterday—yesterday!" They exclaimed, "Thou hast been damned for above five thousand years, and thou sayest yesterday!" Again he replied: "Oh, if you did but know what eternity means, you would well understand that five thousand years are, by comparison, not even a moment." If an angel were to say to one of the damned: Thou shalt leave Hell, but when as many ages have passed as there are drops of water, leaves on the trees, and grains of sand on the seashore, he would rejoice more than a beggar on hearing that he was made a king. Yes, because all those ages will pass away; even be they multiplied an infinite number of times, and Hell will still be only beginning. Each one of the damned would make this agreement with God: "Lord, increase my pain as much as Thou wilt; make it last as long as Thou pleasest; put but a limit to it, and I am content." But no, this limit will never be. The trumpet of Divine justice will sound forth in Hell nothing but, *"Forever forever! never! never!"*

The damned will ask of the devils, "What hour of the night is it? (Isaias 21:11). When will it end? When will these trumpets, these cries, this stench, these flames, these torments end?" And the answer will be: "Never! never!" "And how long will they last?" "Forever! forever!" Ah, Lord, give light to those many blind ones, who, when entreated not to lose their souls, reply: "If I go to Hell in the end, well, I must have patience!" O God, they have not patience to bear a little cold, to remain in a hot room, to endure a blow; and yet they will have patience to live in a sea of fire, trampled upon by devils, and abandoned by God and by everyone, for all eternity!

AFFECTIONS AND PRAYERS

O Father of Mercies, Thou forsakest not those who seek Thee! (*Psalms* 9:11). In past times I have so often turned my back on Thee, and Thou hast not abandoned me; do not abandon me now that I seek Thee. I repent, O Sovereign Good, of having made such small account of Thy grace as to exchange it for a mere nothing. Behold the wounds of Thy Son; hear their cry, beseeching Thee to pardon me; and do Thou pardon me. And Thou, my Redeemer, bring always to my remembrance the torments Thou hast suffered for me, the love Thou hast borne me, and my ingratitude, by which I have so often deserved Hell, in order that I may unceasingly bewail my offenses against Thee, and live always inflamed with Thy love. Ah, my Jesus, how shall I not burn with love for Thee, when I consider that I deserve to have been burning in Hell long ago, there to burn for all eternity; and that Thou hast died to deliver me from it, and with so much mercy hast delivered me. If I were in Hell, I should now hate Thee, and be obliged to hate Thee forever; but I love Thee, and will love Thee forever. I hope for this through the merits of Thy blood. Thou lovest me, and I also love Thee. Thou wilt always love me, if I do not leave Thee. Ah, my Saviour, save me from the misfortune of ever leaving Thee, and then do with me what Thou wilt. I deserve every chastisement; and I accept of it, that Thou mayest deliver me from the chastisement of being deprived of Thy love. O Mary, my refuge, how often have I condemned myself to Hell, and thou hast delivered me from it! Ah, deliver me from sin, which alone can deprive me of the grace of God, and condemn me to Hell!

CONSIDERATION XVIII

The Remorse of the Damned

"Their worms dieth not." Mark 9:47

FIRST POINT

By this worm that dieth not, is meant remorse of conscience, says St. Thomas, by which the damned will be eternally tormented in Hell. In many ways will conscience gnaw the heart of the reprobate; but the three most grievous things will be, to reflect upon the trifles for which they have lost their souls; the little they were required to do to be saved; and finally, the great good they have lost. The first sting, then, of the damned will be, to think for what trifles they have lost their souls. After Esau had eaten of the pottage of lentils, for which he had sold his birthright, the Scriptures tell us, that through grief and remorse at his loss he cried aloud: "He roared out with a great cry." (*Gen.* 27:34). Oh, how will the damned cry and roar aloud, when they reflect that for a few momentary and poisonous gratifications they have lost an eternal kingdom of joys, and are forever condemned to a continual death! Therefore will they weep far more bitterly than Jonathan wept, when he found himself condemned to death by his father Saul for having eaten a little honey (*1 Kings* 14:43). O God, what a torment will it be to the damned to see then the cause of their damnation! Even at present, what does our past life appear to us but a dream, a moment? And what will the fifty or sixty years they have lived on this earth appear to those who are in Hell, when they find themselves in the abyss of eternity; in which, after a hundred or a thousand millions of years, their eternity will still be only beginning? But why do I say fifty years of life? Fifty years perhaps all passed in pleasure? And does the sinner perchance, who lives without God, always

enjoy himself in his sins? How long do the pleasures
of sin last? They last a few moments; and all the rest
of the time of that man who lives at variance with
God is a time of pain and bitterness. Now, what will
these moments of pleasure appear to the poor lost soul?
And, especially, what will that one last sin appear
which has been the cause of his damnation? Then will
she exclaim, For a miserable brutal pleasure, which
lasted but a moment, and vanished like air almost as
soon as possessed, I shall have to remain to burn in
this fire, despairing and abandoned by all, as long as
God shall be God, for all eternity.

AFFECTIONS AND PRAYERS

O Lord, enlighten me, that I may know the injus-
tice I have done Thee, and the eternal punishment I
have deserved by offending Thee. My God, I feel a great
grief for having offended Thee; but this grief consoles
me. If Thou hadst sent me to Hell, as I deserved, this
remorse would be the Hell of my Hell, considering for
what trifles I have lost my soul; but now this remorse
(I repeat) consoles me, because it encourages me to
hope for my pardon; since Thou hast promised it to all
that repent. Yes, O my Lord, I repent of having out-
raged Thee; I embrace this sweet pain; nay, I pray Thee
to increase it, and to preserve it in me till the hour of
death, that I may always bitterly weep over the displeasure I have caused Thee. My Jesus, pardon me. O
my Redeemer, who, through pity for me, hadst no pity
on Thyself, condemning Thyself to die in torments to
deliver me from Hell, have mercy on me. Grant, then,
that whilst my remorse keeps me ever afflicted for
having offended Thee, it may at the same time inflame
my whole soul with the love of Thee, who hast so much
loved me, and so patiently borne with me; and who
now, instead of chastising me, enrichest me with lights
and graces. I thank Thee, O my Jesus, and I love Thee;
I love Thee more than myself; I love Thee with my

whole heart. Thou canst not despise one who loves Thee; I love Thee; banish me not from Thy presence. Receive me, then, into Thy favour, and never again permit me to lose Thee. Mary, my Mother, accept me as thy servant, and bind me to thy Son Jesus. Pray to Him to pardon me, and to give me His love, and the grace of perseverance until death.

SECOND POINT

St. Thomas says that the principal pain of the damned will be, to see that they have lost their souls for nothing, and that they might so easily have gained the glory of Heaven, had they chosen. Their chief grief shall be that they are damned for nothing, whilst they could have most easily obtained everlasting life. The second sting of conscience, then, will be to reflect upon the little they were required to do to be saved. A lost soul appeared to St. Humbert, and told him that this precisely was the greatest pain by which he was tormented in Hell, to think for what trifles he had damned himself, and how little he had to do in order to be saved. Then will the miserable soul say: Had I mortified myself by not looking at such an object, had I conquered that human respect, had I shunned that occasion, that companion, that conversation, I should not now be lost. Had I gone to confession every week, had I been assiduous in joining in the duties of my confraternity, had I read every day such a spiritual book, had I recommended myself to Jesus Christ and to Mary, I should not have fallen again into sin. I so often resolved to do these things, but I did not keep to my resolutions; or I commenced to keep them, and afterwards neglected them; and therefore am I lost.

The pain of this remorse will be aggravated in the damned by the examples they had before them of virtuous friends and companions, and still more by the gifts bestowed on them by God, that they might save their souls: gifts of nature, such as good health; gifts of fortune, talents that the Lord had given them, to make a good use of, and thereby to become saints; gifts, moreover, of grace, so many lights, inspirations, calls, and so many years granted to repair what they had done amiss: but in that miserable state to which they are reduced, they will see that there is no more time for reparation. They will hear the angel of the Lord cry out, and swear, "by Him that liveth for ever and ever, that there should be time no longer." (*Apoc.* 10:5-6). Oh, what cruel daggers will all those graces which it has received be to the heart of the poor damned soul, when it shall see that the time for repairing its eternal ruin is past forever! It will then say, weeping with the companions of its despair, "The harvest is past, the summer is ended, and we are not saved." (*Jer.* 8:20). Alas, will it cry out, if I had labored for God as much as I did for my damnation, I should have become a great saint! And now what remains for me but remorse and pains, which will torment me for all eternity?" Ah, this thought will torment the damned more than the fire and all the other tortures of Hell: I might have been forever happy, and now I must be miserable forever and ever.

AFFECTIONS AND PRAYERS

Ah, my Jesus, how hast Thou been able to bear with me so long? I have so often turned my back on Thee, and Thou hast not ceased to seek after me. I have so often offended Thee, and Thou hast pardoned me; and again I have offended Thee, and Thou hast again pardoned me. Ah, give me a share in that sorrow, which Thou didst feel in the garden of Gethsemane for my sins, which caused Thee to sweat blood! I repent, my dear Redeemer, of having so ill repaid Thy love. Alas, accursed pleasures, I detest and curse you! Through you I lost the grace of my Lord. My beloved Jesus, I now love Thee above all things: I renounce all unlawful gratifications; and I purpose rather to die a thousand times than offend Thee again. Ah, by that tender affection with which Thou didst love me on the Cross, and didst offer up Thy divine life for me, give me light and strength to resist temptations, and to have recourse to Thy aid, whenever I am tempted. O Mary, my hope, thou art all-powerful with God; obtain for me holy perseverance, and the grace never to separate myself again from His holy love.

THIRD POINT

The third remorse of the damned will be, to see the great good which they have lost. St. John Chrysostom says, that they will be more tormented by the loss of Heaven than by the very pains of Hell: "They are tormented more by Heaven than by Hell." The unhappy Elizabeth, queen of England, said, "God give me forty years to reign, and I renounce Paradise." The wretched woman had her forty years; but now that her soul has left this world, what says she? She is surely no longer of the same mind. Ah, now how must she not find herself afflicted and in despair at the thought, that for these forty years of an earthly reign, accompanied with many fears and perplexities, she has lost for all eternity the kingdom of Heaven! But that which will most afflict them for all eternity will be, to know that they have lost Heaven, and God their sovereign good, not through ill fortune, or the malevolence of others, but through their own fault. They will see they were created for Paradise; that God placed in their hands the choice of obtaining for themselves life or death eternal: "Before man is life and death, good and evil: that which he shall choose shall be given him." (*Ecclus.* 15:18). Thus they shall see that it was in their own power, had they pleased, to make themselves eternally happy; and they will see that themselves, by their own free choice, have chosen to cast themselves into that pit of torments, from which they will never be able to escape, and from which none will ever endeavor to deliver them. They will see among the saved so many of their companions, who were placed in the same, and perhaps even greater, dangers of sin; but because they knew how to restrain themselves, and to recommend themselves to God, or if they fell, knew how to rise again and to give themselves to God, they saved their souls: but they, the damned, because they would not put an end to sin, they have come to Hell to finish it in that sea of torments, without hope of ever being able to apply a remedy.

My brother, if in past times you have also been so foolish as to choose to lose Heaven and God for the sake of some miserable pleasure, endeavor, now that there is yet time, speedily to apply a remedy. Do not continue in your folly. Tremble lest you have to bewail your misfortunes in eternity. Who knows but that this consideration which you are now reading may be the last call that God will give you? Who knows, if you do not now change your life, whether the next mortal sin you commit, God will not abandon you, and for this send you to suffer for all eternity amid that crowd of fools who are now in Hell confessing their mistake? "Therefore have we erred;" but they confess it in despair, seeing that it is without remedy. When the devil tempts you to sin again, think of Hell; have recourse to God, to the Blessed Virgin: the thought of Hell will deliver you from Hell: "Remember thy last end, and thou shalt never sin." (*Ecclus.* 7:40); because the thought of Hell will make you have recourse to God.

AFFECTIONS AND PRAYERS

Ah, my Sovereign Good, how many times have I lost Thee for a mere nothing, and have deserved to lose Thee forever! But the words of the Prophet console me: "Let the heart of them rejoice that seek the Lord." (*Psalms* 104:3). I must not, therefore, despair of recovering Thee, my God, if I seek Thee with all my heart. Yes, my Lord, now I sigh for Thy grace above every other good. I am content to be deprived of everything, even of life, rather than see myself deprived of Thy love. I love Thee, my Creator, above all things; and because I love Thee, I repent of having offended Thee. O my God, once lost and despised by me, pardon me speedily; and grant that I may find Thee, since I desire never more to lose Thee. If Thou receivest me again into Thy friendship, I will leave all things, and give myself up to the love of Thee alone. This I hope for through Thy mercy. Eternal Father, hear me for the love of Jesus Christ; pardon me, and give me the grace never to separate myself from Thee again: for if I again wilfully lose Thee, I ought justly to fear that Thou wilt abandon me. O Mary, O peace-maker of sinners, bring me into peace with God; and then hold me fast under the mantle of thy protection, that I may never lose Him again.

CONSIDERATION XIX

On Perseverance

"He that shall persevere to the end, he shall be saved."　　Matthew 24:13

First Point

St. Jerome says, "that many begin well, but few are those that persevere."[96] Saul, Judas, Tertullian, began well; but they ended badly, because they did not persevere in virtue: "In Christians it is not the beginnings, but the end, that is required."[97] The Lord, continues the saint, does not require only the beginnings of a good life, but the end also; it is the end that will obtain the reward. St. Bonaventure says that the crown is given to perseverance alone: "Only perseverance is crowned." For this reason, St. Laurence

Justinian calls perseverance "the gate of Heaven." He, then, who does not find the gate cannot enter Paradise My brother, you have now quitted sin, and justly hope that you have been pardoned. You are, then, the friend of God; but know that you are not yet saved. And when will you be saved? When you have persevered to the end: "He that shall persevere to the end, he shall be saved." You have begun a good life; thank God for it: but St. Bernard warns you that the reward, though promised to him who begins, is only given to him who perseveres: "The prize, promised to beginners, is given to those who persevere."[98] It is not enough to run for the prize; but we must run until we obtain it: "So run that you may obtain," says the Apostle.

You have already put the hand to the plough, you have begun a good life; but now more than ever fear and tremble: "With fear and trembling work out your salvation." (*Phil.* 2:12). And why? Because if (which God forbid) you look behind, and turn back to a bad life, God will declare you to be excluded from Paradise: "No man putting his hand to the plough, and looking back, is fit for the kingdom of God." (*Luke* 9:62). Now, by the grace of God, you avoid the occasions of sin, you frequent the sacraments, you make your meditation every day: happy are you, if you continue to do so, and if Jesus, when He shall come to judge you, shall find you so doing: "Blessed is that servant whom, when his Lord shall come, he shall find so doing." (*Matt.* 24:46). But do not believe that now, because you have set yourself to serve God, temptations are at an end, or will be wanting. Listen to what the Holy Ghost says to you: "Son, when thou comest to the service of God, prepare thy soul for temptation." (*Ecclus.* 2:1). Know that now more than ever must you prepare yourself for battle; because your enemies—the world, the devil, and the flesh—will arm themselves now more than ever against you to make you lose what you have gained. Denis the Carthusian says, that the more anyone gives himself up to God, the more does Hell strive to overcome him: "The more bravely a man strives to serve God, so much the more fiercely does the enemy rage against him." And this is stated clearly enough in the Gospel of St. Luke: "When the unclean spirit is gone out of a man, he walketh through places without water, seeking rest; and not finding, he saith: I will return into my house whence I came out. Then he goeth and taketh with him seven other spirits more wicked than himself, and entering in, they dwell there. And the last state of that man becomes worse than the first." (*Luke* 11:24-26). The devil, when he is cast out of a soul, finds no repose, and does all he can to enter into it again; he calls his companions to his aid, and if he succeeds in re-entering, the second ruin of that soul will be far greater than the first.

Consider, then, what arms you must make use of to defend yourself against these enemies, and to keep yourself in the grace of God. There is no defence but prayer against being overcome by the devil. St. Paul tells us that we have not to fight against men of flesh and blood like ourselves, but against the powers of Hell: "Our wrestling is not against flesh and blood, but against principalities and powers." (*Eph.* 6:12). And he wishes to warn us that we have not the strength to resist such powerful enemies, but that we stand in need of the help of God: we can do all things with the Divine assistance: "I can do all things in him who strengtheneth me." (*Phil.* 4:13). So spoke St. Paul, and so ought each one of us to speak. But this aid is only given to such as ask for it by prayer: "Ask, and you shall receive." Let us not trust, then, to our resolutions; if we put our confidence in them, we shall be lost. When we are tempted by the devil, let us place all our confidence in the help of God; recommending ourselves at such times to Jesus Christ and to the most holy Mary. And this especially when we are tempted against chastity; because this is the most terrible of all temptations, and is the one by which the devil gains the most victories. We have not the strength to preserve chastity; God must give it to us. Solomon said, "And as I knew that I could not otherwise be continent, except God gave it . . . I went to the Lord, and besought him." (*Wis.* 8:21). In such temptations we must instantly have recourse to Jesus Christ and to His holy Mother, and frequently invoke their most holy names. He who does so, shall conquer; he who does not it, shall be lost.

Affections and Prayers

"Cast me not away from Thy face." Ah, my God, do not cast me away from Thy face; I well know that Thou wilt never abandon me, if I am not the first to forsake Thee: but this I fear from past experience of my own weakness. O Lord, Thou must give me the strength I require against Hell, which aims at having me again as its slave. I ask it of Thee for the love of Jesus Christ. Establish, O my Saviour, a perpetual peace between Thyself and me, never to be broken for all eternity; and therefore give me Thy holy love. "He who loveth not, remaineth in death; whoso loves Thee not is dead." From this miserable death Thou must save me, O God of my soul. I was lost, Thou knowest it well. It was Thy goodness alone that brought me back into my present state, and I hope to continue in Thy grace. Ah, my Jesus, through that bitter death Thou didst endure for me, never permit me wilfully to lose Thy grace again. I love Thee above all things. I hope to be forever bound by this holy love, and so bound to die; and to live so bound for all eternity. O Mary, thou art called the Mother of Perseverance: this great gift is dispensed through thy hands; I ask it of thee, and through thee I hope for it.

Second Point

Let us now see how we must conquer the world. The devil is a great enemy, but the world is worse. If the devil did not make use of the world and of bad men (by which is meant *the world),* he would not gain such victories as he does. Our Redeemer does not warn us so much to be on our guard against devils as against men: "Beware of men." (*Matt.* 10:17). Men are often worse than devils, because the devils are put to flight by prayer, and by invoking the most holy names of Jesus and Mary; but if bad companions tempt a person to sin, and he reply by some spiritual word, they do not fly, but tempt him the more; they laugh at him, call him a miserable man of no education, and good for nothing; and when they can say nothing else, they call him a hypocrite who affects sanctity. To avoid such reproaches and derision, certain weak souls unhappily associate with these ministers of Lucifer, and return to the vomit. My brother, be assured that if you wish to lead a good life, you must endure the jeers and contempt of the wicked: "The wicked loathe them that are in the right way." (*Prov.* 29:27). He who leads a bad life cannot bear the sight of those who live well; and why? Because their life is a continual reproach to him; and he would therefore wish all to imitate himself, that he might not feel that pain of remorse which the good life of others causes him. There is no help for it (says the Apostle); he who serves God must be persecuted by the world: "All that will live godly in Christ Jesus shall suffer persecution." (*2 Tim.* 3:12). All the Saints have been persecuted. Who more holy than Jesus Christ? and the world persecuted Him, even to cause Him to bleed to death upon a cross.

There is no remedy for this, because the maxims of the world are all contrary to those of Jesus Christ. That which the world esteems, is called folly by Jesus Christ: "For the wisdom of this world is foolishness with God." (*1 Cor.* 3:19). On the contrary, the world calls folly that which is esteemed by Jesus Christ—such as crosses, sufferings, and contempt: "For the word of the cross to them indeed that perish is foolishness." (*1 Cor.* 1:18). But let us console ourselves; for if the wicked curse and blame us, Almighty God blesses and praises us: "They will curse, and thou wilt bless." (*Psalms* 108:28). Is it not enough for us to be praised by God, by Mary, by all the Angels, by the Saints, and by all good men? Let us, then, leave sinners to talk as they please, and let us continue to please God, who is so grateful and faithful to those who serve Him. The greater the repugnance and the opposition we meet with in doing good, the more shall we please God, and the greater will be our merit. Let us imagine that there is none in the world save God and ourselves. When the wicked jeer at us, let us recommend ourselves to the Lord; and, on the other hand, let us thank God that He gives us that light which He withholds from these unhappy men, and so let us go our way. Let us not be ashamed of appearing as Christians; for if we are ashamed of Jesus Christ, He protests that He will be ashamed of us, and to have us at His right hand at the Day of Judgment: "For he that shall be ashamed of me and of my words, of him the son of man shall be ashamed, when he shall come in his majesty." (*Luke* 9:26).

If we wish to be saved, we must resolve to suffer, to overcome ourselves, nay, to do violence, to ourselves: "Strait is the way that leadeth to life." (*Matt.* 7:14); "The kingdom of heaven suffereth violence, and the violent bear it away." (*Matt.* 11:12). He who does no violence to himself will not be saved. There is no help for it, since if we wish to practice virtue, we must act in opposition to our rebellious nature. We must especially do violence to ourselves at the beginning, in order to root out bad habits and to acquire good ones; because, when once a good habit is formed, the observance of the Divine law becomes easy, nay, even sweet. The Lord said to St. Bridget, that whoever in the practice of virtue endures with patience and courage the first pricks of the thorns, will find the thorns turn into roses. Be careful, therefore, dear Christian; Jesus Christ says now to you what He said to the paralytic: "Behold, thou art made whole; sin no more, lest some worse thing happen to thee." (*John* 5:14). Understand, says St. Bernard, if you should unhappily relapse, your ruin will be greater than in all your previous falls: "You hear that to relapse is worse than to fall." Wo, says the Lord, to those who take the way of God, and then depart from it: "Wo to you, apostate children." (*Isaias* 30:1). These are punished as rebels against the light: "They have been rebellious against the light." (*Job* 24:13). And the punishment of these rebels, who have been favored by God with a great light, and then are unfaithful to Him, is to remain blind, and so to end their life in their sins: "But if the just man turn himself away from his justice . . . shall he live? all his justices which he has done, shall not be remembered . . . in his sin he shall die." (*Ezech.* 18:24).

AFFECTIONS AND PRAYERS

Ah, my God, I have often deserved such a punishment, since I have many times forsaken sin through the light which Thou gavest me, and then have miserably returned to it! I thank Thy infinite mercy for not having abandoned me in my blindness, and left me wholly deprived of light, as I deserved. How great, then, O my Jesus, are my obligations to Thee; and how ungrateful should I be, were I again to turn my back upon Thee! No, my Redeemer, "I will sing Thy mercies forever." I hope, during the remainder of my life and for all eternity, to sing forever and to praise Thy great mercies, by always loving Thee, and never to be again deprived of Thy grace. The great ingratitude which I have hitherto shown Thee, and which I now detest and curse above every other evil, will serve to make me always weep bitterly over the injuries I have done Thee, and to inflame me with love of Thee, who, after my many offenses against Thee, hast bestowed on me such great graces. Yes, I love Thee, O my God, worthy of infinite love. From this day henceforth Thou shalt be my only love, my only good. O Eternal Father, through the merits of Jesus Christ, I ask of Thee final perseverance in Thy grace and in Thy love. I know, indeed, that Thou wilt grant it whenever I ask Thee for it. But who can assure me that I shall be careful to beg this perseverance of Thee? Therefore, my God, I ask Thee for perseverance, and the grace always to ask for it. O Mary, my advocate, my refuge, and my hope, obtain for me, by thy intercession, constancy in always asking of God the grace of final perseverance. By the love thou bearest to Jesus Christ. I beseech thee to obtain it for me.

THIRD POINT

We now come to the third enemy, which is the worst of all, that is, the flesh; and let us see how we must defend ourselves against it. In the first place, by prayer; but this we have already considered above. In the second, by avoiding the occasions of sin; and this we will now ponder well. St. Bernardine of Sienna says, that the greatest of all counsels, nay, as it were the foundation of religion, is the counsel to avoid sinful occasions: "Among the counsels of Christ there is one most celebrated, and as it were the foundation of religion, to avoid the occasions of sin." The devil once confessed, being compelled to do so by exorcisms, that of all sermons that which is most displeasing to him is the sermon on avoiding the occasion of sin; and with reason, for the devil laughs at the resolutions and promises of a repentant sinner if he does not quit dangerous occasions. Occasions, especially in regard of sensual pleasures, are as a bandage over the eyes, which prevent a person from seeing either the resolutions he has made, or the lights he has received, or the eternal truths; in short, they make him forget all, and as it were blind him. The cause of the ruin of our first parents was, not avoiding the occasion of sin. God had forbidden them even to touch the fruit: "God hath commanded us (said Eve to the serpent) that we should not eat, and that we should not touch it." (*Gen.* 3:3). But she heedlessly "saw," "took," and "eat it." First, she began to look at the apple, then she took it in her hand, and then she eat it. He who wilfully puts himself into danger shall perish in it: "He that loveth danger shall perish in it." (*Ecclus.* 3:27). St. Peter says, that the devil "goeth about seeking whom he may devour." Hence, says St. Cyprian, what does he do to re-enter into a soul from which he has been banished? He goes and seeks for an occasion: "He explores whether there be any side through whose entrance he might penetrate his way." If the soul allow herself to be induced to throw herself into the occasion, the enemy will enter into her afresh, and will devour her. The Abbot Guerric, moreover, remarks, that Lazarus rose from the dead bound: "He came forth bound hand and foot;" and rising thus he died again. Unhappy he, this author means, who rises from sin, but rises bound with the occasions of sin: such a one, though he rise, will nevertheless turn back and die. He, then, who wishes to be saved must leave, not only sin, but also the occasions of sin, that is to say, such a companion, such a house, such a connection.

But you will say, I have now changed my life, and I have no longer a bad intention with that person, nor even a temptation. I answer: It is related, that in Africa there are certain bears which go in pursuit of apes. The apes, when they see the bears, save themselves by climbing up the trees; but what does the bear? He stretches himself under the tree, and pretends to be dead; and when he sees the apes come down, he rises, carries them off, and devours them. So does the devil; he makes the temptation appear to be dead; but when the person comes down and throws himself into the occasion, he causes the temptation to come to life again, and it devours him. Oh, how many miserable souls who were in the practice of prayer, frequented the holy Communion, and who might have been called saints, by throwing themselves into the occasions of sin have remained the prey of Hell! It is related in ecclesiastical history, that a holy matron who devoted herself to the pious work of burying the martyrs, once found one who was not yet dead; she took him to her house, he recovered; but what happened? Through the proximate occasion these two saints, as they might be called, first lost the grace of God and afterwards the faith.

The Lord commanded Isaias to preach that every man is grass: "Cry, all flesh is grass." (*Isaias* 40:6). Upon which St. Chrysostom makes this reflection: "Is it possible that grass should not burn when placed in the fire? "Place a lighted candle amongst hay, and then dare to say that it will not be burned." And in like manner, says St. Cyprian: "It is impossible to be surrounded by flames and not to burn."[99] Our strength, the prophet warns us, is as the strength of tow placed in the fire: "Your strength shall be as the ashes of tow." (*Isaias* 1:31). Solomon likewise says, that he would be a fool who should pretend to walk on live coals without being burned: "Can a man walk upon hot coals, and his feet not be burnt?" (*Prov.* 6:28). In the same way is he mad, who pretends to put himself into the occasions of sin without falling. We must therefore fly from sin as from the face of a serpent: "Flee from sins as from the face of a serpent." (*Ecclus.* 21:2). We must avoid, says Gualfridus, not only the bite, not only the touch, but even the approach of a serpent: "Avoid even its touch, its very approach." But that house, you say, that friendship, is for my interest. But if you well see that that house is the road to Hell for you ("Her house is the way to hell," *Prov.* 7:27), there is no help for it— you must quit it, if you would be saved. Even were it your right eye, says the Lord, if you see that it be the cause of your damnation, you must pluck it out and cast it far away from you: "If thy right eye scandalize thee, pluck it out and cast it from thee." (*Matt.* 5:29). And mark the expression *abs te;* you must cast it away, not near to you, but far from you: which is as much as to say, you must remove every occasion. St. Francis of Assisi said, that the devil tempts spiritual persons who have given themselves to God very differently from the way in which he tempts the wicked: at first he does not try to bind them with a cord, he is content with a hair; then he binds them with a thread, then with a string, and at last with a cord, and so at length he draws them into sin. He, therefore, who would be free from this danger must from the very first despise those hairs, those occasions, those salutations, presents, notes, and the like. And for those especially who have contracted a habit of impurity, it will not be sufficient to avoid the proximate occasions; if they do not avoid even the remote, they will fall back again into sin.

It is necessary for everyone who really desires to save his soul, frequently to renew his resolution never to separate himself from God, and to be frequently repeating with the Saints, "Let all be lost, provided God is not lost." But it is not enough to resolve never again to lose Him; it is necessary also to take the means for not losing Him. The first of these is, to avoid the occasions, of which we have already spoken; the second is, to frequent the sacraments of Confession and Communion. Dirt does not reign in that house which is often swept. By Confession the soul is kept pure, and not only obtains the remission of sins, but also the strength to resist temptations. The Communion is called heavenly bread, because, as the body cannot live without earthly, so the soul cannot live without this heavenly food: "Unless you eat the flesh of the son of man, and drink his blood, you shall not have life in you." (*John* 6:54). On the other hand, eternal life is promised to him who frequently eats of this bread: "If any man eat of this bread, he shall live for ever." (*Ibid.* 5:52). On this account the Council of Trent calls the Communion "that medicine by which we are delivered from our daily faults, and are preserved from mortal sin."[100] The third means is, meditation or mental prayer: "Remember thy last end, and thou shalt never sin." (*Ecclus.* 7:40). He who keeps before his eyes the eternal truths of death, judgment, and eternity, will not fall into sin. In meditation God enlightens us: "Come ye to him and be enlightened." (*Psalms* 33:6). There He speaks to us, and makes us understand what we have to avoid and what to do: "I will lead her into solitude, and there I will speak to her heart." (*Osee* 2:14). Meditation, moreover, is that blessed furnace in which is enkindled the Divine love. "In my meditation a fire shall flame out." (*Psalms* 38:4). Besides, as we have already frequently observed, if we wish to preserve ourselves in the grace of God, it is absolutely necessary to be always praying and asking for the graces we require: he who does not make mental prayer, hardly prays, and by not praying he will certainly be lost.

We must therefore make use of the means of salvation and of leading a well-ordered life. In the morning, on rising, make the Christian acts of thanksgiving, love, offering, and good resolution, with prayers to Jesus and Mary that they may preserve us that day from sin. After meditation, hear Mass. During the day, spiritual reading—the Visit to the Blessed Sacrament and to the Divine Mother. In the evening, the Rosary and Examination of Conscience. Go to Communion several times in the week, according to the advice of your director, which you should steadily follow. It would be also highly profitable to make a retreat in some religious house. You should also honor the Blessed Virgin by some special devotion—by fasting, for example, on Saturday. She is called the Mother of Perseverance, and she promises it to him who serves her: "They that work by me shall not sin." (*Ecclus.* 24:30). Above all, ask always of God the gift of holy perseverance, especially in time of temptations, and invoke then more frequently the holy names of Jesus and Mary as long as the temptation lasts. If you do this, you will certainly be saved; if you do it not, you will certainly be lost.

AFFECTIONS AND PRAYERS

My dear Redeemer, I thank Thee for these lights and means which Thou givest me to know myself and save my soul. I promise Thee that I will perseveringly make use of them. Give me Thy help, that I may be faithful to Thee. I see that Thou dost wish to save me, and I desire to be saved, chiefly to gratify Thy heart, which so earnestly desires my salvation. I will not, O my God, any longer resist Thy love towards me. This love it was which made Thee bear with me with so much patience while I was offending Thee. Thou invitest me to love Thee; and I desire nothing more. I love Thee, O Infinite Good. Grant, I pray Thee, by the merits of Jesus Christ, that I may never again be ungrateful to Thee. Either put a stop to my ingratitude, or let me die. O Lord, Thou hast begun the work, do Thou now perfect it: "Confirm, O God, that which Thou hast wrought in us." Give me light, give me strength, give me love. O Mary, who art the treasurer of graces, do thou assist me. Proclaim me to be thy servant, as I desire to be, and pray to Jesus for me. First the merits of Jesus Christ, and then thy prayers, must save me.